REBEL SCIENCE

Written by Dan Green

Illustrated by David Lyttleton

STERLING CHILDREN'S BOOKS

New York

STERLING CHILDREN'S BOOKS
New York

An Imprint of Sterling Publishing
1166 Avenue of the Americas
New York NY 10036

STERLING CHILDREN'S BOOKS and the distinctive
Sterling Children's Books logo are trademarks of
Sterling Publishing Co., Inc.

First Sterling edition published in 2016.

First published in 2014 by Weldon Owen Limited.
www.weldonowenpublishing.co.uk

Weldon Owen Limited is part of the
Bonnier Publishing Group
www.bonnierpublishing.com

© 2014 Weldon Owen Limited
Text © 2014 Dan Green
Written by Dan Green
Illustrated by David Lyttleton
Produced for Red Lemon Press by DUTCH&DANE

ISBN 978-1-4549-1945-2

Manufactured in China

Lot #: 10 9 8 7 6 5 4 3 2 1

12/15

www.sterlingpublishing.com

CONTENTS

Sir Isaac Newton

WHAT IS THIS THING CALLED SCIENCE?

Science is a way of looking at, investigating, and understanding our universe. Since we started to ask "How does that work?" it has taken us on an amazing journey.

SCIENCE IS:
CURIOSITY

Our natural curiosity makes us try to find out things and understand them. What we find out can sometimes be shocking and even very scary. Scientists use experiments, math, and imagination to make sense of things. It is one of the only subjects where it's OKAY to be wrong—it's all part of the process. Where else can you say this?

SCIENCE IS:
DISAGREEMENT

There are "laws" that scientists invent to describe the Universe, but—like all the best rules—they are there to be broken. Science works by "consensus." That means building up a picture of how stuff works that everybody can agree on. Sometimes, scientific rebels cook up new ideas that go against the consensus, leading to some almighty arguments!

Louis Godin

Pierre Bouguer

Charles Marie de La Condamine

START HERE!

Mary Anning

BOOM AND BUST!

There are two main methods that we use to explore the universe—theory and experiment. We get theories (ideas) about the way things work and then find ways of testing them out. The best theories must be "testable," even if that means poking into a black hole with a ruler!

Albert Einstein

Johannes Kepler

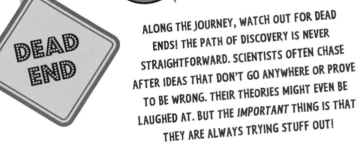

SCIENCE IS:
DISCOVERY

We don't know it all yet.

Not by a long shot! There are many things that science still has not fully explained, including mass, gravity, time, consciousness, and the "dark matter" that seems to make up most of the stuff in the universe, but which we cannot even see. Phew! It's a never-ending path of discovery.

John Gurdon

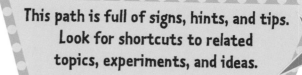

This path is full of signs, hints, and tips. Look for shortcuts to related topics, experiments, and ideas.

DEAD END

ALONG THE JOURNEY, WATCH OUT FOR DEAD ENDS! THE PATH OF DISCOVERY IS NEVER STRAIGHTFORWARD. SCIENTISTS OFTEN CHASE AFTER IDEAS THAT DON'T GO ANYWHERE OR PROVE TO BE WRONG. THEIR THEORIES MIGHT EVEN BE LAUGHED AT. BUT THE *IMPORTANT* THING IS THAT THEY ARE ALWAYS TRYING STUFF OUT!

EXIT AHEAD

THE HISTORY OF SCIENCE IS A WILD RIDE, WITH UNEXPECTED TWISTS AND TURNS, UNSEEN REVERSES, AND TRICKY DEAD ENDS. SO, STEP THIS WAY ... AND KEEP YOUR WITS ABOUT YOU AS YOU BEGIN YOUR JOURNEY OF SCIENTIFIC DISCOVERY.

SCIENCE IS:
A LONG JOURNEY

Science is for people who are interested in the world around them. Science is for those who like to ask questions, and aren't afraid to ask "Why?" and "How?" when people say they know how things work. When he was in school, John Gurdon's science teacher thought his work was "a disaster" and that his ideas about becoming a scientist were "ridiculous." In 2013, Gurdon won a Nobel Prize, so don't ever be put off by how long something takes to figure out, or by what other people tell you!

Walter Alvarez

Luis Alvarez

THE STORY OF THE SOLAR SYSTEM

With stars in their eyes, these guys sat and watched the universe go by, carefully noting down what they saw. They were among the very first of the rebel scientists. Their ideas about the solar system conflicted with the accepted beliefs of their time.

POLISH SUN KING:
NICOLAUS COPERNICUS

Moving the Earth Copernicus (1473–1543) had a different view of the solar system. He said that our planet is spinning, the Moon orbits Earth, Earth orbits the Sun, the Sun's at the center of the solar system, and that a tilted orbit causes Earth's seasons. He was really worried that his ideas would cause trouble, so he waited until the very end of his life before letting people see his book on the subject.

DOWN-TO-EARTH FELLOW:
PTOLEMY
At the center of things

If you watch the night sky, the stars and planets seem to wheel slowly overhead. There's no feeling of movement for us on the surface, so it was only natural for early astronomers to think that Earth lay at rest—right at the center of everything. Everybody knew that Ptolemy (ca. 90–168ce) was one of the best stargazers, so they kinda just went along with what he said. His Earth-centered theory was the longest unchallenged scientific theory of all time.

SHEN KUO

In the 11th century, Chinese super-brain Shen Kuo watched the shadows the Earth made on the Moon and figured that both the Moon and the Sun are ball-shaped. He also spotted that the Moon only reflects light (it doesn't produce it). All the while he improved designs for shiny new pieces of astronomy equipment.

Ptolemy was a super-duper thinker, but he wasn't always right. Check out his ideas about light on page 36.

THE HUMAN CALCULATOR:
JOHANNES KEPLER

Solar sums In 1609, math whiz Johannes Kepler struck gold. He was in charge of the top observatory of the day in Prague, now in the Czech Republic. He number-crunched his way through stacks of Tycho Brahe's astronomical data and figured out how the planets move in space. His two laws of planetary motion showed that the planets follow elliptical (oval-shaped) orbits around the Sun. This matched Tycho's own observations.

COSMIC SUPERSTAR:
TYCHO BRAHE

Going supernova Tycho lived on his own private island, in a house built for him by the king of Denmark. He had a pet elk and threw the wildest parties! He lost his nose in a fight, so he had a couple of metal ones made. Tycho made superb observations of the night sky, and in 1572 he spotted a "supernova" (the explosive death of a massive star). His discovery proved that the heavens weren't simply fixed and unchanging.

ROUTE-FINDER

Join the Dinomania on page 16.
Feel the force of Newton's laws of gravity and motion, which predicted the movement of planets, on page 25.
Consider the possibility of life on other planets on page 35.

FACE-OFF: GALILEO GALILEI VS. THE ROMAN INQUISITION

PLANETS COLLIDE

You want a rebel, huh? Galileo's your go-to guy. Punchy, persuasive, and prepared to stand up for what he thought was right, Gal got into a big, heavyweight fight with the Catholic Church over our planet's place in the cosmos. It wanted Earth to be at the center of everything, but Galileo (1564–1642) wasn't afraid to tell it like it is—even if it got him into some very hot water. What a champ!

BURNING BRUNO

Being a rebel isn't easy. In 1600, Giordano Bruno was tied to a pole and burned alive. The Italian scientist supported Copernicus's Sun-centered solar system ideas. The Roman Inquisition executed him because he refused to deny his claim that every star is a sun—and probably has planets around it—just like our own.

THE ORIGINAL SCIENCE REBEL:

GALILEO GALILEI

"You can't tell me what to think!"

I've used my new telescope to look outside the Earth. I've seen mountains on the Moon. POW! I've seen rings around Saturn. BAM! Okay, so I thought they were 'ears' at first … but the fact that Jupiter has moons totally proves that not everything orbits the Earth. BOOM! Earth moves around the Sun and you'll never get me to say otherwise!"

THE ITALIAN STALLIONS:

THE CATHOLIC CHURCH

"Hey, we're the good guys! We're a big organization and can handle a little 'free thinking'. But this revolutionary wants to revolve everything and it's making our heads spin. Worse still, he's making us look *stupid!* So don't be surprised if we don't applaud at your rebellious ideas—we're more likely to clap you in irons and roast you over a hot fire! Get ready for the Holy Roman takedown! **"**

THE ROMAN INQUISITION

From the mid-16th century until the early 19th century, the inquisitors enforced the law of the Church—they told people what to think and steam rolled over anyone who didn't do what they said. They pressed, tortured, and took no prisoners—except in the case of Galileo. After his run-in with the boys from the Inquisition, he was kept under house arrest until he died.

A DANGEROUS WORD

HERESY. *Shudder!* Enough to send shivers down even a brave person's spine, heresy was the word the Catholic Church used to describe any ideas that didn't fit in with its world view.

Five planets are easy to see in the night sky. Ancient astronomers knew all about these and they used them to find out about Earth's position. But for those who were prepared to look, there was more out there waiting to be discovered. Space was about to get much bigger.

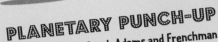

PLANETARY PUNCH-UP

Englishman John Couch Adams and Frenchman Urbain Le Verrier believed that an as-yet-unknown planet might be causing "wobbles" in Uranus's orbit. Using brain-busting math they both successfully predicted Neptune's location in 1846—but kicked off an almighty science spat over who did it first.

SIBLING SPOTTERS:
THE HERSCHELS

New horizons In 1781, for the first time in history, the known universe expanded. Brother-and-sister team William and Caroline Herschel added the planet Uranus to the solar system—the first planet to be spotted using a telescope.

PLANET GEORGE

William called his planet "George" in honor of the king of England, George III (and got 340 dollars for the favor). Was Willy kind of slimy or a smart cookie? You decide!

BETWEEN 1895 AND 1908, PERCIVAL LOWELL, A BRAINIAC FROM BOSTON, SPIED ON SOME ALIENS BUILDING CANALS ON MARS FROM HIS SWANKY NEW OBSERVATORY IN ARIZONA. PROBLEM WAS, HE WAS ACTUALLY LOOKING AT NATURAL FEATURES OF THE MARTIAN LANDSCAPE!

DEAD END

DEDICATED DUDE:
CLYDE TOMBAUGH
Fantastic flickers

Percival Lowell began the hunt for "Planet X" in 1906. After 7,000 hours of staring down his "blink comparator"—which flicked rapidly between two photos of the same region of space—Clyde Tombaugh finally spotted the moving dot in 1930. A cold and gloomy world, Pluto was named after the Roman god of the underworld by an 11-year-old girl called Venetia Burney.

DWARF-CATCHER:
MICHAEL E. BROWN
A new family of planets

In 2005, Mike Brown and his team—at the Palomar Observatory in California—found a "tenth planet" in the depths of space, three times farther away from the Sun than Pluto is. Since there might be lots more of these small planets, it was decided to refer to them as "dwarf planets." Currently, there are five. Largest to smallest, their names are Eris, Pluto, Haumea, Makemake, and Ceres.

KEY DISCOVERIES

* The Earth and the Moon are spheres.
* The Earth and other planets orbit (travel around) the Sun.
* The stars are not fixed in position.
* Stars are "born." They live and die.
* Planetary orbits are not circular, they are elliptical (oval-shaped).
* There is more to the solar system than we can see with the naked eye. There are distant planets, dwarf planets, comets, and other objects, too.

EXIT AHEAD

IN 2013, VOYAGER 1—LAUNCHED IN 1977—LEFT THE SOLAR SYSTEM BEHIND. WITH ENOUGH FUEL TO LAST UNTIL 2025, THE TINY PROBE NOW STREAKS ACROSS INTERSTELLAR SPACE, CROSSING UNCHARTED PARTS OF THE UNIVERSE WITH EVERY MILE IT TRAVELS.

THE STORY OF THE EARTH

What's the shape of the planet we live on? How big is it, and how heavy? Has it always looked like this? These earthy rebels had their feet on the ground, their heads in the clouds, and answered questions that most people thought were crazy even to ask!

BATTLE OF THE BULGE

In 1738, three Frenchmen set sail for South America to measure the bulge around Earth's middle. The expedition was a total washout—the team members got their measurements wrong, ran out of money, argued, and stopped speaking to each other. Bouguer (left), Godin (middle), and La Condamine (right) were even beaten to the answer by another crew!

GEOGRAPHY GIANT:
ERATOSTHENES

Earth's girth! In 240BCE, while watching boats sail out to sea and disappear beyond the horizon, Eratosthenes—head of the world's biggest library at Alexandria, Egypt—guessed that Earth was shaped like a ball. Nicknamed "Beta," he devised a cunning, and stunningly accurate, experiment to measure a small segment of the Earth's surface. Using his results, he then estimated the entire distance around our planet's middle.

DEAD END

EDMOND HALLEY (1656–1742) WAS AN AWESOME ASTRONOMER AND A SCIENCE SUPERSTAR, BUT HE WENT TOO FAR IN 1692 WHEN HE SAID THAT THE EARTH WAS HOLLOW. HE DIDN'T STOP THERE, EITHER. HE SAID THE PLANET WAS MADE OF FOUR HOLLOW SPHERES (THE LARGEST ON THE OUTSIDE), EACH ONE BRIGHTLY LIT INSIDE AND FULL OF LIFE. WEIRD.

HUTTON'S BIG HUNCH

Scottish "rock star" James Hutton (1726–97) had a burning desire to find out why the countryside looks like it does. He rode far and wide on his horse, searching for clues. As well as a sore backside, he got his answer: Earth shows "… no vestige of a beginning, no prospect of an end," as he put it. In other words, Earth's natural processes are slow and its surface features take a very long time to form. Our planet is an ancient place indeed.

GREENHOUSE GEEZER:
SVANTE ARRHENIUS

Hot stuff! In 1837, radical Swiss geologist Louis Agassiz (1807–73) proposed that the planet's temperature has changed over time, with "ice ages" having occurred in the past. In 1896, Swedish chemist Svante Arrhenius worked out that "greenhouse gases" keep the Earth warm by trapping some of the Sun's heat in the atmosphere. Svante was also the first to predict how carbon dioxide from burning fossil fuels would lead to global warming.

SUPER-SHY GUY:
HENRY CAVENDISH

Weight of the world Science was the only thing Henry Cavendish cared about. In 1797–98, dressed in a baggy coat and a 100-year-old hat, he painstakingly measured the gravitational attraction between two small spheres made of lead. He then used the results to calculate the density (compactness) of our planet. To make sure his own mass didn't mess up the experiment, Cavendish put his equipment in a separate room and made his observations from outside, using a telescope.

Turn to page 16 to find out how fossils helped scientists make sense of Earth's history.

Introducing:

THE AGE OF THE EARTH

Things are getting feisty at the fair as six scientists set up their stalls. Each one has a pet theory to present to customers like you! So come one, come all: It's time to hear some righteous, riotous, rebellious, and ridiculous ideas.

IT'S IN THE BIBLE

First up is Irish Archbishop James Ussher, who—in 1650—calculated the age of Earth by adding up the histories of all the families in the Bible. He believed that the Good Book was the complete record of Earth's history, and that it proved that the planet was a sprightly 5,500 years old.

IT'S IN THE DIRT

In 1830, building on the work of James Hutton, English "rock legend" Charles Lyell thought that 75,000 years didn't give enough time to lay down the great thicknesses of soil and sediment on the planet. How much time does it take, then, Charlie? "Unimaginably vast amounts!" said Charlie.

IT'S IN THE IRON

Breaking with the Bible, a radical French count called Comte de Buffon tried physics. He decided that the Earth had cooled from a red-hot ball—so, in 1778, he based his calculations on the cooling rates of iron. This put the planet at 75,000 years old. Brainiac or buffoon? You decide!

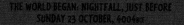

THE WORLD BEGAN: NIGHTFALL, JUST BEFORE SUNDAY 23 OCTOBER, 4004BCE

PLANET EARTH IS 75,000 YEARS OLD

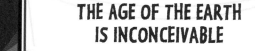

THE AGE OF THE EARTH IS INCONCEIVABLE

AGE-OLD ARGUMENTS

Deciding how to divide time into geological periods was enough to divide friends. In 1834, best buddies Adam Sedgwick and Roderick Murchison fell out over which rocks belonged in the Cambrian period and which belonged in the Silurian. They never spoke to each other again.

IT'S IN THE COOLING

"Nonsense! Rot! Poppycock!" In 1862, Lord Kelvin decided to put a stop to the foolishness and fuzzy thinking being sold by Chuck Lyell. Getting back to solid, sensible physics, he estimated that about 98 million years were most probably needed for the planet to cool from its hot, sticky start.

IT'S IN THE ELEMENTS

Kelvin hadn't counted on radioactive elements in the Earth, which add extra heat when they decay (break down), thus slowing the planet's cooling rate. Ernest Rutherford's first stab, with Bertram Boltwood, used radioactive uranium as a "natural clock" to help measure Earth's age. By 1907, they had calculated it as being between 250 million and 1.3 billion years old.

CLAIR CAMERON PATTERSON

By 1956, radiometric dating—the measurement of radioactive decay to calculate the age of things—was getting pretty accurate. Clair Patterson used this process to give a date to the Canyon Diablo meteorite, which crash-landed in Arizona, about 50,000 years ago. Knowing that this rock must have formed at the same time as our planet, Patterson wanted to know its age. He calculated it as 4.54 billion years old, which is now the accepted age of our planet. Hooray! Wild cheers!

THE PLANET TOOK AT LEAST 98 MILLION YEARS TO COOL

THE EARTH COULD BE AS OLD AS 1.3 BILLION YEARS

THE EARTH IS APPROXIMATELY 4.54 BILLION YEARS OLD!!

XENOPHANES OF COLOPHON

Wandering bard and scribbler of risqué poems, Xenophanes (ca. 560–478BCE) stumbled on an upsetting idea: that fossils in rocks are the remains of living things. His examination of fossils also led him to believe that dry land must have been under the sea at some point in the past.

On these pages, we dig a little deeper in our quest to learn all we can about our home planet. Come and meet the bone-rattlers who weren't afraid to shake things up and get a little dirty in the process.

COPROLITE QUEEN:
MARY ANNING

She sells seashells ... Mary Anning (1799–1847) was the top dinosaur hunter of her day. Women weren't supposed to be scientists in those days, but Mary didn't let that stop her. Tough as a tyrannosaur, she pulled marvel after marvel from the cliffs of Lyme Regis in the UK. She was also the first to spot what "coprolites" really were: fossilized dino dung!

DINOMANIA

In 1841, Richard Owen invented a new name for the group of majestically large, extinct reptiles that kept turning up as fossils in rocks. He called them *dinosaurs*, which means "terrible lizards." The dinosaurs may have died out, but dinomania was definitely here to stay!

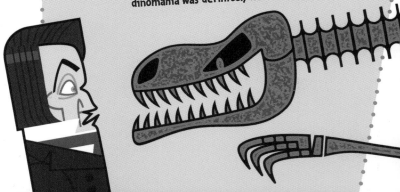

COMPARATIVELY CLEVER:
GEORGES CUVIER

Mammoth task Cuvier (1769–1832) was the world's leading expert in animal anatomy. People would send him bones, and he could identify which animal they came from. By comparing elephant jawbones with fossilized mammoth chompers, this bone-man realized that some animals no longer exist—they've died out and become extinct. Oh dear, oh dear!

HOMINID HUNTERS:
THE LEAKEYS

Bones! Dinners with fossil hunters Louis and Mary Leakey were always rib-tickling. In the 1950s, this married couple went looking for the ancestors of humans. They discovered many fossils of extinct hominids (relatives of humans)—including the famous *Homo habilis*, or "handyman"—suggesting that humans evolved from apes and originally came from East Africa.

KEY DISCOVERIES

* Earth measures 24,901 miles (40,075km) around its bulging middle.

* Earth is a lot older than we thought.

* Our planet has not always been warm, and the global climate has changed over time.

* Fossils are the remains of living things from past times.

* The animals and plants alive today are not the only ones that have lived on this planet.

* Humans have ancestors that looked similar to apes.

ROUTE-FINDER

Take a scenic detour and swing over to page 35, where you can enjoy an overview of the fairly rebellious idea that all life has a common ancestor (distant relative).

DUO OF DOOM:
LUIS AND WALTER ALVAREZ

An idea with impact In 1980, a dad-and-son team came up with a reason for the mass extinction that occurred 65 million years ago. An asteroid strike, with the power of 200 million thermonuclear bombs, meant a "big goodbye" to dinosaurs and three-quarters of all animals and plants. Luis and Walt's "fire from the sky" theory was considered totally far-out, until a crucial piece of evidence was found in Mexico—an impact crater 110 miles (180km) wide and 12 miles (20km) deep.

FACE-OFF: ALFRED WEGENER VS. A WHOLE WORLD OF OPPOSITION

EARTH-SHAKERS

These rabble-rousers broke new ground when they challenged the old ideas about how mountains form. Deep-rooted theories often seem set in stone and scientists don't like letting them go—as was proven by this epic butting of heads, which lasted 50 years! Wegener's revolutionary idea of drifting continents, first proposed in 1912, needed more evidence to back it up. Here, then, are the geological giants who moved mountains.

GIGGLING GEEKS:
THE DOUBTERS

"**What garbage, what nonsense!** We all know that mountains are wrinkles formed as the Earth cools. Only a fool would think the planet's a giant jigsaw puzzle. Where, we ask you, is the force powerful enough to push enormous slabs of rock across the surface? No, there's no way this simple weatherman can prove his *ridiculous* idea! "

MID-OCEAN RIDGES

During the 20th century, evidence slowly built up to support Wegener's theory. The killer discovery came in the 1950s, when ocean-floor surveys found high ridges that run like seams down the middle of the oceans. Molten rock oozes out of these volcanic mountain ranges, pushing plates of the Earth's crust apart—at about the same speed as your fingernails grow.

THE PUZZLER:
ALFRED WEGENER

"**The continents are moving!** The edges of Earth's landmasses look like they once fit together in one big 'supercontinent.' Also, the same fossils are found on lands that are now separated by a vast ocean. And there's evidence of glaciers in the tropics and tropical swamps in polar parts. Clearly, the continents have moved around. "

THERMAL THINKER:
ARTHUR HOLMES

" I always liked Alf's idea ... So, in 1929, I came up with a theory that might make it work. What if 'plates' of solid crust floated on a gooey mantle? Then, thermal convection currents in the mantle might push the continents across the Earth's surface. **"**

RIDGE-RIDER:
HARRY HESS

" I took all these ideas and added them to my 'sea-floor-spreading' model of 1962. New crust is made at mid-ocean ridges and recycled in the deep ocean trenches. And this all acts like a conveyor belt that shunts the continents around. **"**

KING OF THE CRUST:
MAURICE EWING

" In 1947, I was sent to explore a mysterious ridge in the middle of the Atlantic Ocean. Here, I found that the ocean crust is thinner, newer, and made of totally different rock to continental crust. Fascinated by this, I've spent most of my life crisscrossing the oceans to gather my beloved crusty data. **"**

THE TECTONIC PLATES

In 50 years, Wegener's ideas had gone from ridicule to respect. What resulted was John Tuzo Wilson's theory of "plate tectonics." Earth is broken up like Humpty Dumpty's shell. There are 16 large tectonic plates and 80 smaller microplates. The interiors of the plates are stable. The exciting stuff, such as earthquakes and volcanoes, mostly happens around the edges, where the plates bump and grind past each other.

GLORY BOYS:
VINE, MATTHEWS, AND MORLEY

" This victory is ours! We put the icing on Harry Hess's sea-floor-spread cake, in 1963, with our discovery of 'magnetic reversal stripes' on mid-ocean ridges (shown here, left). Finally, we had the key piece of evidence to demonstrate continental drift. *Yahoo!* **"**

THE STORY OF THE ATOM

Just when the story of the stuff that makes up matter was looking nicely tied up, along came a bunch of rebels who ripped up the rule book! This series of shocking discoveries revealed a new, "subatomic" world—smaller than the atom itself.

ALPHA MALE:
JAMES CHADWICK

Neutral zone Sharp-suited scientist Jimmy Chadwick—acting on a total hunch—bombarded beryllium with radioactive alpha particles in 1932. This dislodged never-seen-before particles from the atomic nucleus. The neutral "neutrons" (subatomic particles without an electrical charge) act like a glue that holds the central parts of an atom together, stopping the positively charged protons from blowing it apart.

ELECTRON EGGHEAD:
J.J. THOMSON

Negative vibes Until 1897, scientists thought that the atom was the smallest part of matter. Then, zap-happy J.J. Thomson spotted tiny particles streaming off the negative terminal of a high-voltage Crookes tube, or vacuum tube. These negatively charged "electrons" were attracted toward the positively charged plates. They were the first subatomic particles ever found.

J.J. KNEW THAT ATOMS WERE NEUTRAL. AND, SINCE ELECTRONS ARE SO LIGHT, HE FIGURED THAT THEY WERE LIKE RAISINS INSIDE A HEAVY, POSITIVELY CHARGED ATOM—ARRANGED LIKE THE FRUIT IN A "PLUM PUDDING."

DEAD END

REACTIONARY GUY:
LEÓ SZILÁRD

Great balls of fire! In 1933, Hungarian genius Szilárd was walking in London, UK, when he figured out how to make a nuclear chain reaction work. A controlled chain reaction can generate nuclear power inside a reactor. But if it's an *uncontrolled* reaction… BOOM! Leó was eager to build an atomic bomb, so that we could understand its power. But he was NOT thrilled to see one being used to fight wars.

THE EN-ERGIZER:
ENRICO FERMI

Critical mass On December 2, 1942, the world's first nuclear reactor—built on a squash court at the University of Chicago—went critical. With no radiation shielding or cooling system, Fermi's "pile" was built to produce plutonium for Robert Oppenheimer's bomb (right). The risky reactor also delivered a brand-new source of energy, now widely used today.

KEY DISCOVERIES

* **Atoms are NOT the smallest parts of matter that exist.**
* **Electrons are negatively charged, subatomic particles that are easily "knocked off" atoms.**
* **Most of the mass of an atom is in a tiny, central nucleus (containing positive protons and neutral neutrons) that is orbited by electrons.**
* **Neutrons can split the atom's nucleus and create a powerful chain reaction.**

A DEADLY PROJECT

The Manhattan Project was the world's biggest, most expensive, and most top-secret scientific program. Run by J. Robert Oppenheimer during World War II, it built the world's first nuclear bomb in 1945. When he saw the awful explosion it created, Oppenheimer was reminded of a Hindu verse, "I am become Death, the destroyer of worlds."

Introducing: THE ATOMIC BAKE-OFF

Welcome to tonight's show—where scientists try out their top recipes for making an atom. Yes, instead of eggs and flour, tonight we're cooking with protons, neutrons, and electrons. The challenge is to produce an atomic model that doesn't fall apart.

THIS RANKS AS ONE OF THE ALL-TIME MOST SURPRISING RESULTS IN PHYSICS!

THE GOLD FOIL CHALLENGE

Geiger, Marsden, and Rutherford were all atomic masterchefs. In 1909, they bombarded a thin strip of gold leaf (thin gold foil) with radioactive alpha particles. They expected that the positive parts of Thomson's "plum pudding" atom would deflect the particles a little, but some of them bounced straight back.

Ernest Marsden

Ernest Rutherford

Most particles passed straight though or were deflected just a little bit.

THOMSON'S "PLUM PUDDING"

J.J. Thomson created the science sensation of 1897 when he discovered the electron. Then he used his scientific kitchen skills to bake the "plum pudding" model, also known as the "blueberry muffin" model, in 1904. Here, his light electrons are folded into a dense dough of positive charge, like raisins in a cake. Not a bad effort, but ultimately a little too heavy.

J.J. Thomson

Sheet of thin gold foil

The particles made a bright flash when they hit the surrounding screen.

Radioactive source of alpha particles

Some particles ended up over here.

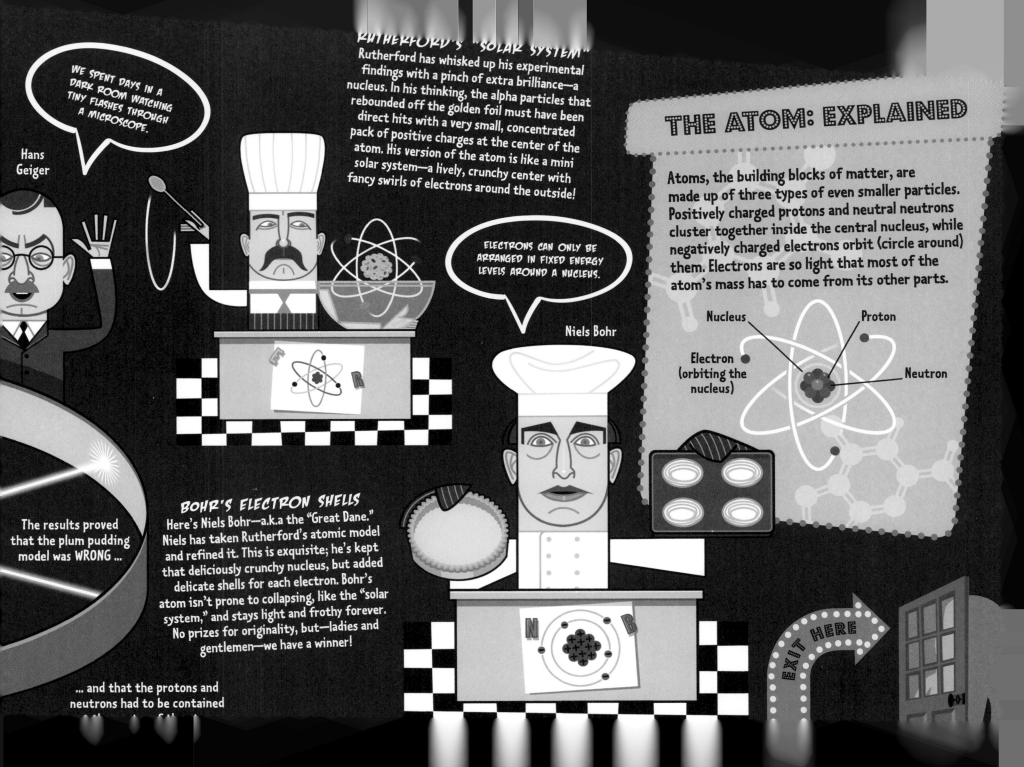

THE ATOM: EXPLAINED

Atoms, the building blocks of matter, are made up of three types of even smaller particles. Positively charged protons and neutral neutrons cluster together inside the central nucleus, while negatively charged electrons orbit (circle around) them. Electrons are so light that most of the atom's mass has to come from its other parts.

Nucleus

Proton

Electron (orbiting the nucleus)

Neutron

RUTHERFORD'S "SOLAR SYSTEM"

Rutherford has whisked up his experimental findings with a pinch of extra brilliance—a nucleus. In his thinking, the alpha particles that rebounded off the golden foil must have been direct hits with a very small, concentrated pack of positive charges at the center of the atom. His version of the atom is like a mini solar system—a lively, crunchy center with fancy swirls of electrons around the outside!

> WE SPENT DAYS IN A DARK ROOM WATCHING TINY FLASHES THROUGH A MICROSCOPE.

Hans Geiger

> ELECTRONS CAN ONLY BE ARRANGED IN FIXED ENERGY LEVELS AROUND A NUCLEUS.

Niels Bohr

BOHR'S ELECTRON SHELLS

Here's Niels Bohr—a.k.a the "Great Dane." Niels has taken Rutherford's atomic model and refined it. This is exquisite; he's kept that deliciously crunchy nucleus, but added delicate shells for each electron. Bohr's atom isn't prone to collapsing, like the "solar system," and stays light and frothy forever. No prizes for originality, but—ladies and gentlemen—we have a winner!

The results proved that the plum pudding model was WRONG ...

... and that the protons and neutrons had to be contained

EXIT HERE

THE STORY OF FORCES

Forces change things. They push and pull on stuff to move it, speed it up, slow it down, squeeze it, stretch it, and bend it out of shape. A dynamic gang of hotheads dared to ask what made things move—and uncovered the secrets of these invisible powers.

MOVING HEAVEN AND EARTH

Archimedes was King Hiero II's main science dude. Among his many discoveries, this Greek genius showed that the longer a lever is, the more force you can produce with it. He used to boast that he could move the world with a long enough lever!

GOLDEN BOY:
ARCHIMEDES

Splash! Archimedes (ca. 287 – ca. 212bce) had to find out if the king's goldsmith was cheating by mixing silver into the royal crown. Silver is less dense than gold, so an equal weight of it should fill more space. While taking a bath, Archie noticed that you can measure an object's volume (the space it takes up) by how much water it displaces (sloshes out). "EUREKA!" ("I have found it!") he cried.

LEVER POWER

Most levers, such as scissors and nutcrackers, are force-boosters—converting a small force over a long distance into a BIG push over a short distance. However, there's a third class of lever that SHRINKS a force to allow precise control. Tweezers are a good example of this.

DEAD END

BRAINY ARISTOTLE CLAIMED THAT HEAVY THINGS FALL FASTER THAN LIGHT THINGS. "OKAY," SAID GALILEO, "WHAT ABOUT A 22LB (10KG) WEIGHT TIED TO A 2.2LB (1KG) WEIGHT? WOULD THE LIGHTER WEIGHT SLOW THE FALL OF THE HEAVIER ONE, OR WOULD THE COMBINED WEIGHT FALL FASTER THAN BOTH OF THEM INDIVIDUALLY?" GOOD QUESTIONS, EH?

ARISTOTLE'S IDEAS HAD BEEN AROUND FOR YEARS. HIS FOLLOWERS TAUGHT THEORIES SUCH AS "OBJECTS NEED CONSTANT FORCE TO KEEP THEM MOVING"—CLAIMING THAT ARROWS, FOR EXAMPLE, WILL KEEP TRAVELING ONCE THEY HAVE LEFT THE BOW BECAUSE AIR GATHERS BEHIND THEM AND PUSHES THEM ALONG. WRONG AGAIN! WHEN COOL ISAAC NEWTON CAME ALONG, ARISTOTLE QUICKLY WENT OUT OF STYLE.

DEAD END

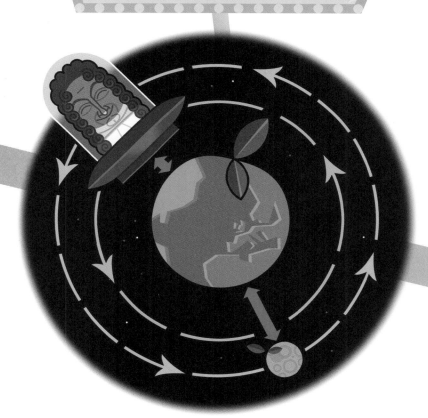

Gravity was the first fundamental force to be discovered. Turn to page 28 to find out when the others were found.

ROCK 'N' ROLL STAR:
GALILEO GALILEI

They couldn't arrest his mind While under house arrest in the 1630s (see page 9), the Big G worked on the problem of "things falling." By timing objects as they rolled down slopes, he calculated that all objects fall at the same speed—a theory eventually proved by astronauts on the Moon hundreds of years later. He also added the fact that objects need a force in order to change their speed.

A FORCE TO BE RECKONED WITH:
SIR ISAAC NEWTON

Laws of motion Isaac's mom wanted him to be a farmer, but he rebelled and became a scientist—one of the greatest of all time! Between 1665 and 1667, while avoiding the Great Plague, Newt worked on some rules governing forces and motion, as well as the force that makes things with mass attract each other—gravity! LAW ONE: things keep going or stay still until a force acts on them. LAW TWO: The more force there is acting on an object, the more acceleration that object has. LAW THREE: Every action (or force) has an equal and opposite reaction.

FACE-OFF: ISAAC NEWTON VS. ROBERT HOOKE

BEAT BOXERS

Back in the 17th century, an epic war of words took place between two titans of physics—Isaac Newton (1643–1727) and Robert Hooke (1635–1703). And now, for one night only, these two verbal gladiators are BACK, going head-to-head in an epic rap battle. They're spittin' rhymes and waxing lyrical about their greatest scientific achievements. Let's see which one can shake it down the hardest!

Calculus

Optics

Gravitation

SPACE EXPLORATION

[I]saac Newton's three gilt-edged laws of motion (see page 25) [sho]wed how forces combine to make things move. They stood [unc]hallenged for more than 200 years. Teamed together with his law of universal gravitation, they sent men to the Moon and back, and space probes to the very edges of our solar system.

NEWT'S BEST BITS:

SIR ISAAC NEWTON

"I lay down the law! I rolled out the best tunes in physics—invented a new mathematics and the laws that sent men into space. I figured out the nature of light, an' showed you how it splits into rainbows. The heavens dance to my tune—yeah, I guess you could say I've seen farther than most. Listen up, MC Hooke, I'm the Gravitational Guru and I'm takin' you down!**"**

BOB'S HOTTEST HITS:

ROBERT HOOKE

"Yo, yo, I got the best hooks!

You buried your head in books, but I got down and dirty and took a real look. I was the first pro scientist, the bona fide King of the Lab! I'm the Crown Prince of compression—springs and gases whispered their secrets to me. I built the best microscopes and saw the first cells. Take a swim, Newt, there's only room for one bigwig around here! "

Master of the microscope

Laws of elasticity

Laws on the pressure and volume of gases

THE LONDON MONUMENT

Robert Hooke helped to design and rebuild London, UK, after the Great Fire of 1666. The Monument marks the spot where the fire started, but why stop there? Hooke made it double as a scientific instrument. He gave the column a flip-top lid to turn it into a telescope, and used its hollow shaft to conduct gravity experiments. Monumental!

WHEN BIG BRAINS COLLIDE

Hooke once suggested that Newton had "borrowed" some of his ideas on gravitation. In fact, scholars are still working out which ideas originally came from Hooke and which came from Newton's brain.

The four fundamental forces are the mysterious powers that make our universe tick. Gravity keeps the planets spinning; electromagnetism (EM) governs the properties of materials; the weak force is responsible for radioactivity; and the strong force holds atomic nuclei together. Pretty "fundamental," huh?

BEARDED BRAINIAC:
JAMES CLERK MAXWELL

May the force be with you! Scottish bright spark Maxwell is right up there with Isaac Newton in the All-Time Top 10 of science. In 1861–62, he described how electrical and magnetic fields combine, using just four tricky equations. The amazing EM force keeps things solid, provides light and electricity, and stops the Sun's deadly radiation from wiping out life on this planet.

MAGNETIC PERSONALITY:
HANS CHRISTIAN ØRSTED

Spark of discovery In 1820, Danish scientist Ørsted was fiddling with his electrical equipment when he saw the needle of a compass twitch. He discovered that electric fields can make magnetism, and that magnetic fields can make electricity. We use this fact to generate electricity today, in big power plants.

Maxwell showed that light is a form of EM radiation. Now turn to the Story of Invisible Rays on page 42.

KEY DISCOVERIES

* Levers can multiply forces.
* Heavy and light objects fall at the same speed.
* Objects speed up or slow down only if forces are acting on them.
* Electromagnetism (EM) combines electricity and magnetism.
* Weak force works over tiny distances and combines with EM at high energies.
* Strong force is the strongest fundamental force, while gravity is the weakest.

ELECTRO-WEAKLINGS:

SALAM, GLASHOW, AND WEINBERG

Choose your flavor In the late 1960s, these guys came up with a tasty theory about a "weak force"—at work in the nuclei of atoms—that changes the "flavor" of quarks (the smallest parts of protons and neutrons), turning them from massive quarks into lighter quarks. The weak force plays a crucial part in the nuclear-fusion reaction that keeps the Sun shining.

JOINING FORCES

Super-brainy theoretical physicists are on the trail of a single "superforce." At crazily high energies, all four fundamental forces might become one. Stay tuned for more news.

FORCEFUL FELLOWS:

BARDEEN, FRITZSCH, AND GELL-MANN

Charged up The strong force is a beast: the most powerful force in the universe. It holds the nucleus of atoms together against the EM force. In 1973, these three brainiacs described how quarks stick together inside protons and neutrons because of their "color charge." When the strong force breaks down, the atomic nucleus splits apart and the energy is released in an awesome and terrible nuclear explosion.

THE STORY OF LIFE ITSELF

Life is mysterious. The spark that brings us and other living things to life comes and goes, but what is it and where does it come from? It takes a rebel to tackle these huge questions. For this job, you need a wide-open mind and nerves of steel.

JAN INGENHOUSZ

Solar power Where do plants get the energy to grow? Ingenhousz (1730–99) put plants underwater and watched as bubbles formed on the undersides of their leaves, when in sunlight. In darkness, the bubbles stopped forming. The emerging gas caused a glowing candle to burst into flame—it was oxygen. Ingenhousz worked out that plants trap the energy in sunlight and convert it into food.

ABSOLUTELY ROTTEN:

FRANCESCO REDI

Bad meat BBQ Unafraid of nasty smells, Italian rebel Redi (1626–97) stuffed a dead snake, fish, and beef into jars, covering some of them and leaving others open. The meat in the open jars was soon bubbling over with maggots laid by flies, but the meat in the covered jars was maggot-free. This totally fried the idea that life comes from nonliving things.

DEAD END

SOMETIMES, NEW LIFE SEEMS TO APPEAR OUT OF NOWHERE. PEOPLE USED TO BELIEVE THAT ROTTEN MEAT CREATED FLIES, THAT MICE CAME FROM SWEATY UNDERWEAR, AND THAT SNAKES COULD BE MADE BY PUTTING STRAW INTO A PAIL OF FRESH MILK. INTERESTING IDEAS, BUT VERY, VERY WRONG!

Take a look through Antonie van Leeuwenhoek's awesome microscopes in the Story of Microbes, page 56.

ARE WE ALIENS?

Life has been around on Earth for eons. There is evidence for it in rocks that are more than 3.4 billion years old! But how did it begin? Did it come from space? Turn to page 34 to meet the gang who asked these questions.

MOUSE MAN:
AUGUST WEISMANN

See how they run ... Like the farmer's wife in the nursery rhyme, August Weismann (1834–1914) cut off the tails of 68 white mice to see if the loss of this characteristic gets passed from parent to child. Every one of their 901 kiddie-squeakers had beautifully long tails, proving that things that happen during an organism's life are not inherited by its offspring.

MICROSCOPE MEN:
SCHWANN, SCHLEIDEN, AND VIRCHOW

Cell theory There was nothing that these three German microscope mavericks wouldn't look at. Their persistent peering paid off in the late 1830s, when the trio concluded that all kinds of living things are made of cells. Cells are the smallest units of life, and they can divide (split in two) to make new versions of themselves.

RULES OF LIFE

1. All living things are made up of cells and the products of cells.
2. Cells are the basic building blocks of life.
3. New cells are created by old cells dividing in two.

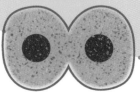

FROGS IN PANTS

All-round science hero Lazzaro Spallanzani always aimed high. In 1776, the Italian scientist decided to find an answer to the question, "Where does new life come from?" To do this, he dreamed up one of the cutest experiments ever attempted.

EXPERIMENTAL SPALLANZANI

Lazzaro Spallanzani (1729–99) had a brilliant imagination. He was interested in everything and found clever ways to test the popular beliefs of the day. As well as reproduction, he investigated microbes and digestion (see page 54). His experimental skills made Spallanzani one of the all-time top rebel scientists.

A "CHICKEN-AND-EGG" PROBLEM

What creates new life? Some thought a woman's egg must come first. Others were certain that a man's sperm holds all the necessary information for the new offspring. To answer this chicken-and-egg scramble, Spallanzani collected a bunch of frogs from his local pond.

THIS GUY'S GOT THE MEASURE OF ME!

"TOADILY," DUDE. HE KNOWS HIS STUFF.

SPALLANZANI'S
AMPHIBIAN FASHIONS

THE TEST

So, why did Spallanzani choose frogs to help him answer this conundrum? Frogs are great for experiments to do with reproduction, because they have see-through eggs—AND they lay these eggs outside the body, in water. Our Italian investigator made little fitted pants for his froggy friends, to see what would happen when the sperm—produced by the males—was prevented from getting to the eggs laid by the females.

A WINNING COMBO

Lazzaro Spallanzani's nifty experiment showed that new life is produced by combining the sex cells of a female and a male. Almost every type of animal reproduces "sexually," which means it needs to bring an ovum (a female egg) into contact with semen (male sperm). Spallanzani even proved that the sperm have to penetrate (get into) the egg. Just getting close to it is not enough.

Sperm and egg: a perfect match

THE RESULT

The "frogs in pants"—those wearing their new pants—produced no new little jumpers. But just to be sure he wasn't jumping to the wrong conclusions, Spallanzani took some sperm out of their pants and found that it was still able to fertilize the eggs. Both the male and female sex cells need to be combined for new life to begin.

HMM, LET'S PUT THIS IDEA INTO PRACTICE.

I'VE GOT THE "JUMP" ON THOSE GUYS... HELLO, LADIES!

OH MY! WHAT LOVELY WARTS.

EXIT HERE

Having figured out that life comes from life, the next question was how it all began—what kick-started life on this planet? In their quest to understand the beginning of all organisms, our rebel gang found that life has lots (and lots) of things in common.

LYNN MARGULIS

Microbe magic Lynn Margulis went out on a limb when she suggested that microbes borrowed DNA from each other—and even went into partnership. She stuck to her guns, and in the 1980s she was proven right. The sunlight-capturing parts of plant cells, and the energy-generating parts of animal cells are "stowaways," and they even have their own DNA!

THE SPARK OF LIFE

It's 1953. Picture the scene: Stanley Miller and Harold Urey are trying to create life in a jar. The idea is that all the ingredients for life were present in Earth's early atmosphere and ocean. A bolt of lightning would awaken it, like Frankenstein's monster. Miller and Urey mixed up a likely-looking brew and zapped it with electricity. The mixture turned pink but made nothing that "organized itself" like living things do.

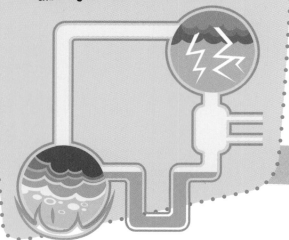

HOT-SPRING HERO:

THOMAS BROCK

Life in the extreme

Working in the boiling-hot springs and acid lakes of Yellowstone National Park in the 1960s and '70s, Brock and his fabulously named assistant, Hudson Freeze, discovered some entirely new kinds of life. They were living there very happily. These gritty, "extremophile" (risk-loving) bacteria showed that life was tougher than previously thought, and that it might have evolved in some pretty hostile environments.

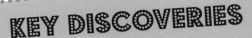

DARWINIAN DUDE:
MICHAEL WIGLER

A shared ancestor Friedrich Miescher, and others, had already shown that DNA is common to all life (see page 62). Then, in 1982, Wigler's yeast microbugs (simple fungi) showed that living things even have some *genes* in common. More than 100 years earlier, Charles Darwin had suggested that all life has a common ancestor (distant relative). The fact that humans still have yeasty genes—from a past, shared ancestor—means that scientists can use the fungus to study how cancers attack humans.

Charles Darwin (1809–82)

DEAD END

IN 1996, SCIENTISTS GOT OVEREXCITED WHEN THEY THOUGHT THEY'D DISCOVERED A FOSSILIZED MICROBE IN A MARTIAN ROCK. IT WAS A FALSE ALARM, BUT MANY THINK THAT LIFE MIGHT HAVE ARRIVED ON COMETS FROM ELSEWHERE IN THE COSMOS.

KEY DISCOVERIES

* All life comes from other life.
* All life gets its energy from the Sun. Plants convert sunlight to make food.
* Every living thing is made up of cells.
* Body cells are not passed on from generation to generation.
* Cells (including ours) contain wriggly passengers that originally came from bacteria.
* Microbes living in extreme or hostile environments could be the planet's oldest life forms.
* Life forms share many of the same genes and DNA.

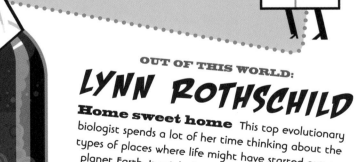

OUT OF THIS WORLD:
LYNN ROTHSCHILD

Home sweet home This top evolutionary biologist spends a lot of her time thinking about the types of places where life might have started out on planet Earth. It might have arrived on a meteorite from space, or grabbed a foothold on "black smokers" (hydrothermal vents) at the bottom of the oceans. Or it might have been "brewed up" in liquid water under a frozen ice cap—something that could also be happening in other parts of the solar system.

Life riding on space rocks

Microbes underneath ice caps

Life around hydrothermal vents

THE STORY OF LIGHT

Light is all around us. By day, it streams in from the Sun, filling the sky. At night, it shines out from electric lights and helps you read books under the covers. But what is this shiny stuff and what on Earth is it made of?

"OLE" TIMER:
OLE RØMER

Quick as light The first person to measure the speed of light was Ole Rømer. In 1676, the Danish astronomer noticed that light reflected from Jupiter's moons took longer to reach his telescope when Earth was farther away from Jupiter. So, although it is very, very speedy, light still takes some time to travel. In fact, it takes between 35 and 52 minutes to travel from Jupiter to Earth (depending on the position of the two planets).

FREE-THINKING GREEK:
PTOLEMY

Laser-beam eyes The first folk to ask about how we see things were the ancient Greeks. Euclid (who was probably born in the 4th century BCE) said that light travels in straight lines—correct, which is why you can't see around corners. Later on, Ptolemy (who died in about 168CE) believed that light shines out of your eyes to help you to see the world. Crazy!

EYE SPY!

Arabic super-brain Ibn al-Haytham (965–1040CE) worked out how light reflects off surfaces, and that you see things because light rays *enter* your eyes. Correct!

Light isn't all about what you can see. Go to page 42 and read about *invisible* rays of light.

REBEL GIANT:
SIR ISAAC NEWTON

Bright ideas As if two major discoveries weren't enough, Isaac Newton came up with dazzling new ideas about light in 1704. This brilliant sci-guy discovered that "pure" white light is, in fact, made up of many different colors. Newt also put forward his belief that light is made up of a stream of tiny particles.

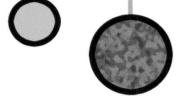

RAINBOW'S END

Newton hit the jackpot when he set out to prove that colors given out by glass prisms (shaped like pyramids) come from light itself, not the prism. He let light shine through a narrow gap in heavy blinds and used a prism to split the beam into a spectrum of colors. Cunningly, Newton blocked out all but one color and aimed it through a second prism. This time, the light didn't split. If the colors came from the prism itself, you'd expect to see a second rainbow. Smart, huh?

ROUTE-FINDER

Hear Galileo boasting about his discoveries on page 8.
Visit the Sun and the planets on pages 6–11.
See atomic scientists baking with particles on pages 22–23.
Watch French rebel Hippolyte Fizeau measure the speed of light on pages 40–41.
Follow Einstein into the Quantum World on pages 72–73.

And then Thomas Young went and rocked Newton's boat with a daring new experiment (see below). After this, total confusion over the nature of light ruled for more than 100 years. Eventually, Albert Einstein opted for the most radical solution: that light is both particles *and* waves.

MANY SCIENTISTS THOUGHT THAT LIGHT MUST NEED SOMETHING TO TRAVEL *THROUGH*. AFTER ALL, SOUND NEEDS MATTER TO JIGGLE AND WATER WAVES NEED LIQUID TO SLOSH. THEY INVENTED A MYSTERIOUS SUBSTANCE CALLED "LUMINIFEROUS AETHER," WHICH HAD TO SEEP INTO EVERY CORNER WHERE LIGHT TRAVELED. PROBLEM WAS, NO ONE COULD FIND ANY SIGN OF IT.

DEAD END

WAVE-MAKER:

THOMAS YOUNG

Interfering When a bigwig like Newton has a favorite theory, most people shut up and agree—but not rebel scientist Thomas Young. His 1800 "double slit" experiment produced "interference" patterns, similar to water waves. This suggested that light travels in waves and NOT as a single beam of particles.

BATTLE OF THE BULBS

In the 1800s, various bright guys, including Humphry Davy, experimented with passing an electrical current through a thin wire, or filament, to make it glow white-hot. What came next was an undignified, underhanded, no-holds-barred scramble to produce an electric lightbulb. To this day, people still fight over whether an American, Thomas Edison, or a Briton, Joseph Swan, invented it first.

Joseph Swan
(1828–1914)

Thomas Edison
(1847–1931)

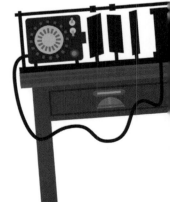

This story is not over yet. Find out more about light—and its role in the universe—in the Story of the Quantum World, page 70.

LASER GAZER:
CHARLES HARD TOWNES

Beam me up! The man with the *toughest* name in science developed futuristic lasers. Lasers get all the packets of light waves to march in sync, producing *intense* beams of a single frequency (color). They are now used everywhere to scan barcodes, read CDs and DVDs, correct eyesight, transmit phone calls and Internet traffic, and even to measure the distance to the Moon! Charlie was awarded the Nobel Prize in Physics in 1964, which he shared with two Russian laser experts.

REBEL LEGEND:
ALBERT EINSTEIN

It's electric! Einstein wasn't afraid to think outside the box. In fact, he more or less flattened the box and threw it away! In 1905, brainy old Albert combined Max Planck's "quantum" ideas (see page 70) with a phenomenon called the photoelectric effect (see page 72). This dynamic new approach suggested that light has properties of both particles *and* waves!

KEY DISCOVERIES

* Light travels in straight lines.
* Vision happens because light enters the eyes (eyes do not give out light).
* White light can be split into a spectrum of colors.
* Light is electromagnetic radiation.
* The speed of light in a vacuum (an airless environment) is 186,282 miles (299,792,458m) per second.
* Light acts both like a wave and like a particle.

Introducing:

THE SPEED OF LIGHT

Light is probably the fastest thing in the universe. It seems to be infinitely fast—seemingly arriving at the same instant it sets off. So, how do you measure something so speedy? Hippolyte Fizeau came up with a plan to put light through its paces.

I HAVE SEEN ZE LIGHT! EET IS A-VERRY FAST!

THE PATH OF LIGHT

Most scientists tried to time light traveling across the vast distances of space, but it is very difficult to measure such distances accurately. Using mirrors, Fizeau bounced his light beam between two hills in Paris, France. He had carefully measured them at 5.364 miles (8.633km) apart.

DISTANCE DIVIDED BY TIME EQUALS SPEED!

HIPPOLYTE "THE FIZZ" FIZEAU

French freestyler Fizeau was the first to invent a technique that gave sensible results for the speed of light. Because light moves so blisteringly fast, he needed to measure its journey over a huge distance—so that he could detect the tiny delays in its travel time.

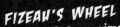

FIZEAU'S WHEEL

Fizeau's 1849 experiment used a toothed wheel, spinning hundreds of times a second, to "chop" a lantern's light into a pulsed beam. He bounced the light off a mirror and adjusted the wheel's speed until the returning beam passed through the next open slot.

CALCULATING SPEED

Speed is the amount of time it takes for something to move a certain distance. So, to figure it out you need measurements for both distance and time. Fizeau's toothed wheel gave him an accurate measurement of time, since he knew how fast the wheel was turning and how far it had moved by the time the pulse of light returned. He also knew the distance the pulse had traveled from hill to hill.

GALILEO'S LAMPS

Galileo was the first to attempt a measurement of light speed, in about 1638. He devised a kind of "light tennis" experiment, in which two people far apart could signal to each other with lanterns. One person would open the door on a lantern, and as soon as the other person saw the light he would open the door on *his* lantern—and then measure the time difference. Of course, no matter how hard they practiced, the beams were too fast for them!

THEN AND NOW

The Fizz's final figure, of 194,676 miles per second, was within a whisker of today's accepted measurement of 182,282 miles (299,792,458m) per second. This was "Fizz-ics" at its best! These days, the speed of light is no longer measured by timing its flight. It's now defined as "... the length of the path traveled by light in a vacuum during a time interval of 1/299,792,458 of a second." Awesome!

THE STORY OF INVISIBLE RAYS

Our peepers are sensitive to only a small portion of the energies of light. How was anyone to know that there were a whole bunch of rays beyond the visible ones? It's time to pull back the blinds and gaze into a totally invisible realm!

ROSE-TINTED REBEL:
WILLIAM HERSCHEL

Seeing red In 1800, William Herschel (first seen on page 10) noticed that sunlight filters on his telescope produced heat—but how much heat depended on their color. Curious, he measured the temperature of each color and found that the hottest part was *beyond* visible red on the spectrum of light. This new kind of light, known as "infrared," is the energy given off by hot objects, stars, flames, and heat lamps.

COOL COSMOLOGIST:
JOHANN WILHELM RITTER

Sun-sensitive Ritter figured that, if there was one set of invisible rays on the red side of the spectrum, there might be a matching set on the *other* side. Bingo! Using silver chloride paper, which darkens when in contact with light, Ritter found invisible "ultraviolet" (UV) rays in 1801. UV light makes things shine in pretty fluorescent colors, but it also gives you sunburn.

Can you name another discovery that was made using a Crookes tube? Go back to page 20 if you can't remember.

Röntgen took an X-ray photograph of his wife's hand in 1895.

X-STATIC FELLOW:

WILHELM RÖNTGEN

Brand X Willy Röntgen's discovery of X-rays, in 1895, was a shock. No one expected it. Röntgen had wrapped his bright Crookes tubes in cardboard to block out the visible light, but his fluorescent screen still glowed. Mysterious rays were passing straight through! X-rays are high in energy, so they can pass through objects, helping us to make images of bones in the body or objects inside bags at airports.

GAMMA GUY:

PAUL VILLARD

Nuclear light beams In 1900, this French physicist discovered the highest-energy light rays while he was investigating radium. Gamma rays come from the breakdown of the nuclei (the central cores) of atoms—and they are extremely dangerous to life. Gamma radiation is released by nuclear bombs and the explosion of massive stars deep in space. It takes a thick lead screen to block these beams.

KEY DISCOVERIES

* Light is part of a larger family of energy waves, called the electromagnetic spectrum.

* Infrared waves lie below the red part of the spectrum.

* Ultraviolet waves lie beyond the violet part of the spectrum.

* X-rays and gamma rays are extra-high-energy forms of light.

THE AMAZING ELECTROMAGNETIC SPECTRUM

Visible light is just a small part of a much wider spectrum of light energy. Radio waves and microwaves are low-energy waves used to carry radio and TV signals, as well as Internet and cell-phone communications. Heat from the Sun is infrared, while high-energy rays—such as ultraviolet, X-rays, and gamma rays—are frazzling. All electromagnetic waves travel at the speed of light.

Radio waves

Microwaves

Infrared

Visible light

Ultraviolet

X-rays

Gamma rays

THE STORY OF THE ELEMENTS

Chemists love to mix things up. Since ancient times they've been preparing perfumes and potions, brewing beer, making glass and soap, and purifying metals. Their quest then turned to finding the simplest substances on Earth: the elements.

GOLDEN WONDER: HENNIG BRANDT

Ur-ine luck! In 1669, German alchemist Hennig Brandt discovered the element of surprise when he went looking for the fabled "philosopher's stone" substance (see below)—in pee. He boiled 50 vats of urine down to a sticky syrup. It would have been a monumentally smelly experiment (you might call it an "ex-smell-iment"), but it resulted in the first chemically isolated element: phosphorus!

ARABIC ALCHEMIST: JÁBIR IBN HAYYÁN

Jabbirish! This Persian potion-sniffer was the world's first chemist. Although his works include nutty recipes for making snakes and scorpions, he also invented lab techniques and glassware that are still used today. Like many scientists of the 8th century CE, Jábir believed in four "classical elements"—air, earth, fire, and water—but he added two of his own, sulfur and mercury.

DEAD END

THE FIRST PEOPLE TO TINKER WITH CHEMICALS WERE CALLED ALCHEMISTS. THEY WENT NUTS FOR THE "PHILOSOPHER'S STONE," A MYTHICAL SUBSTANCE THEY BELIEVED WOULD TURN ONE ELEMENT INTO ANOTHER—PREFERABLY A CHEAP METAL, SUCH AS LEAD, INTO SOMETHING THAT WOULD MAKE THEM FABULOUSLY WEALTHY, SUCH AS GOLD! NO ONE MANAGED THIS MAGICAL FEAT, ALTHOUGH SOME PRETENDED TO KNOW THE SECRET.

THE DOUBTING CHEMIST

One of the original rebel chemists, Robert Boyle (1627–91), absolutely *refused* to believe things just because other people said that's how they were. He said that you shouldn't take things "on authority" (things told to you by others)—you should check things out yourself and never be convinced too easily! That's good advice, Bob.

ROUTE-FINDER

Anatomical addicts fiddle around with the idea of four elements, or "humors," on page 52.

Hans Geiger, Ernest Marsden, and Ernest Rutherford convert one element into another in the great Atomic Bake-Off on pages 22–23.

CELEBRITY CHEMIST:
SIR HUMPHRY DAVY

The man's electric! Darling Davy was the science superstar of his day. He hung out with the top poets and gave public talks to throngs of adoring fans. In the early 1800s, Humphry used newly invented batteries to zap apart compounds and discover several reactive metal elements. The new metals—sodium and potassium—burst into flamboyant flames. Swoon!

THE TOP FIVE
ELEMENT DISCOVERERS

1. Glenn T. Seaborg (9)
2. Jöns Jacob Berzelius (6)
3. Sir Humphry Davy (6)
4. Sir William Ramsay (5)
5. Carl Wilhelm Scheele (5)

FACE-OFF: PRIESTLEY VS. LAVOISIER VS. SCHEELE

BIG REACTIONS

When Joseph Priestley discovered a gassy element in 1774, he described it as, "Five or six times as good as the best common air." It was a breath of fresh air and kept a mouse alive in a glass tube for much longer than usual. Priestley was a self-taught scientist, and he was eager to share his findings—until Antoine Lavoisier took the wind right out of his sails! But did all this huff'n'puff blow away a fairly modest man named Carl Scheele?

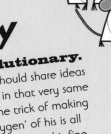

BRITISH FIRE-STARTER:
JOSEPH PRIESTLEY

"I'm a really rowdy revolutionary.
I believe in equal rights and that people should share ideas freely. That way, we'll all be better off. So, in that very same spirit of goodwill, I told my pal Lavoisier the trick of making 'new air.' Next thing I know, this new 'oxygen' of his is all the rage. To be fair, it's a cool name. But making this fine discovery all about 'who was first' is not so cool! That man's head is so inflated, it might float off one day!"

Priestley's "dephlogisticated air" (August, 1774)

O, IT'S GOOD STUFF

Without oxygen (chemical symbol: O), we would die. Divers, astronauts, and firefighters take tanks of this vital stuff to breathe where it's lacking. We need it badly, because it fuels the chemical reactions in our cells. It makes things burn—there's no fire without O_2—and it's a vital part of water (H_2O), too. O, oxygen, what would we do without you?

FRENCH WEIGHT-WATCHER:

ANTOINE LAVOISIER

"Mais pourquoi pas, Priestley? But why not, huh? I made a *proper* science out of chemistry, while you just had a head full of confusion. You see, I work carefully and precisely. My obsession with weighing chemicals—both before and after reactions—showed oxygen for what it really is. It is a gas with which metals *combine* when they burn. Your idea of a precision instrument is a mouse in a jar?! Zat is ludicrous, my friend!**"**

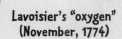

Lavoisier's "oxygen"
(November, 1774)

MODEST SWEDE:

CARL WILHELM SCHEELE

Scheele's
"fire air"
(1771–72)

" Ahem, er, actually... I isolated oxygen before either of these two fame-hungry gasbags, but it's not nice to make a fuss. I told a few friends and finally got around to publishing the news about five years later, in 1777. I've discovered quite a few elements, in fact: molybdenum, tungsten, barium, and chlorine. But I never got the credit for those, either. That's just my hard luck, I guess.**"**

UP, UP, AND AWAY!

All three scientists could have fairly claimed to be the discoverer of oxygen. Scheele did it first, but didn't tell anyone. Priestley got there on his own, but didn't think it was a new substance. Lavoisier most likely "borrowed" Priestley's method of discovery, but saw that the oxygen was a brand-new element and named it! It looks like the trio may all be riding high—it's a tie!

UNHAPPY ENDINGS

Lavoisier was guillotined (had his head cut off), in 1794, during the French Revolution. Scheele also died young, in 1786—killed by some of the nasty chemicals he was working with.

Chemists were getting smarter in their quest, with each new technique producing a fresh batch of elements. In 1803, while observing the chemical reactions of gases, John Dalton figured out that elements are made of different types of atoms, which combine to make chemical compounds.

GAS GIANT:
SIR WILLIAM RAMSAY

Noble discoveries With the help of Morris Travers, William Ramsay (below, left) isolated an entire family of strange, unreactive gases in the 1890s. Distillation is the controlled heating of a liquid to separate the elements in it. By distilling liquid air, Ramsay and Travers found argon, helium, neon, krypton, and xenon. Because they don't react with other elements, these "noble gases" had remained unnoticed. These days, however, they shine brightly out of neon signs and xenon headlamps on vehicles.

DAYDREAM BELIEVER:
DMITRI MENDELEEV

In from the cold When he was in his teens, Mendeleev's mother took him across Russia, from Siberia to Saint Petersburg, trying to find him a good education. Eventually, it paid off. He became the great chemist who wanted to group similar elements into families. Finally, in 1869—inspired by a dream—he arranged them into the "periodic table." His real moment of genius was to leave blank spaces for elements that hadn't been discovered yet.

Elements are different because their atoms have a different structure. Find out more on pages 20–23.

MIXING MADAME:
MARIE CURIE

Stirring achievement Marie Curie (1867–1934) was a trooper. Her motto was, "Never let oneself be beaten down by persons or events." If she saw plenty of tragedy, there was also lots of triumph in her life. With her hubby, Pierre, Marie processed ten tons of a substance called pitchblende to isolate two new elements: radium and polonium. To this day, her notebooks are too radioactive to touch.

The discovery of radioactive elements made people rethink how old our planet is. Find out why on pages 14–15.

KEY DISCOVERIES

* Elements are the simplest forms of matter (stuff).
* Elements make up all the stuff in the universe.
* Elements combine to make compounds.
* Different elements have different types of atoms.
* All atoms of the same element are identical.
* Elements are "lighter" or "heavier" depending on the number of particles in their atoms.
* Elements can be grouped into families with similar chemistry and chemical characteristics.

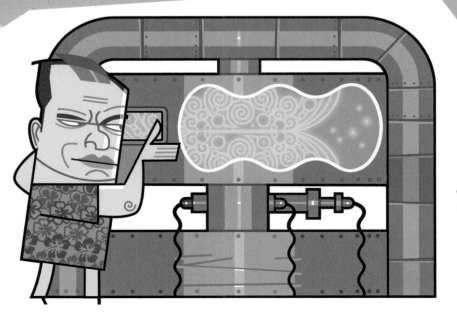

A SMASHING GUY:
GLENN T. SEABORG

Making new elements The number of protons in an element's atoms is known as its "atomic number". Elements "heavier" than atomic number 92 are created artificially inside nuclear reactors and atom smashers. All of them are radioactive, and some are so unstable that they only exist for tiny fractions of a second. Glenn Seaborg has found the most elements (9). He is also the only living person to have had a new element named after him: seaborgium (Sg, atomic number 106).

ARMIES OF ANATOMY

Anatomy. It's the science of the human body: how it fits together and functions. It's a bloody business! In the red corner, we have Galen (ca. 130–210CE), the reigning champ and the most famous surgeon of olden times. In the blue corner is a more recent challenger, Vesalius (1514–64). He came along 1,500 years after Galen, claiming the old dude got it all wrong.

GALEN'S VILE VOLUMES

Galen was a champion scribbler. He wrote 350 books that were still being read 1,500 years after he died. Galen tried to understand what was going on in the body, but lots of his ideas were wrong. He said that blood sloshed back and forth like the tides of the sea, and that the muscles burnt it as fuel.

THE GLADIATOR: GALEN OF PERGAMON

"I'm the all-time greatest!

I'm the personal doctor to Roman emperor Marcus Aurelius, and I've fixed the nasty injuries suffered by gladiators. That's how good I am. No one questions my knowledge of the human body (at least, no one has for over a thousand years). What's wrong with cutting up apes, cows, and pigs to find out how the human body works? It keeps my gladiators on their fighting feet!"

BELGIAN WAFFLER:
ANDREAS VESALIUS

"Don't pull my funny bone.

It's true: they say Galen's the master, but I say he's a medical mix-up. Galen has blended his beasts with his human bodies, and I'm here to cut him down to size. Unlike him, I've opened up plenty of humans, so you could say that I'm a 'cut' above the rest. Just to hammer home my argument, I've made a list of 200 of Galen's greatest mistakes. And now I've got an army of academics on my side. "

THE BUMPER BOOK OF BODIES

Vesalius, the young Belgian prof, started slicing and dicing dead humans in the 1540s. He was determined to find out exactly out how they worked. Using Galen's books to help him, it soon became clear that the great Greek had never actually dissected (cut up) a human! Vesalius employed the best artists to make drawings of the bodies he dissected, and the book he produced in 1543 changed medicine forever.

CUT TO THE CHASE

Andreas Vesalius wasn't the first to dissect a human, but he kicked off a new trend for slicing up dead people to find out how they worked inside.
Dare you read on ... ?

THE STORY OF ANATOMY

We're all fascinated about what goes on inside our insides. These rebel researchers were, too—they opened up the body and peered into it to find out how it works. It's a gory story that gets to the heart of the matter!

CAMILLO GOLGI

He's got some nerve! Italian Camillo Golgi won the 1906 Nobel Prize, in medicine, for inventing a new staining technique. His "black reaction" showed up body cells that were previously invisible. Delicate nerve fibers in the body and neurons in the brain revealed themselves, allowing the nervous system to be mapped and studied for the first time.

IN 1666, CHEMIST ROBERT BOYLE CAME UP WITH THE BRIGHT IDEA OF PUTTING A QUIET, MEEK SHEEP'S BLOOD INTO A MADMAN'S BODY—TO CALM HIM DOWN AND CURE HIM. IT DIDN'T WORK.

DEAD END

DEAD END

REDISCOVERED REBEL:
IBN AL-NAFIS

Ahead of the game Al-Nafis was the chief at a top hospital in Cairo, Egypt. He believed that, although the bloodstream (and heart) is divided into two, blood flows around the whole system—most likely via the lungs. William Harvey (right) is normally credited for this discovery, but a document found in 1924 proved that Al-Nafis was 300 years ahead!

FROM AS FAR BACK AS AROUND 400BCE, PHYSICIANS USED TO THINK THAT THERE WERE FOUR "HUMORS" IN THE BODY—BLOOD, PHLEGM, YELLOW BILE, AND BLACK BILE. THEY FIGURED THAT THE BODY'S ILLNESSES HAPPENED WHEN THESE HUMORS WERE OUT OF BALANCE.

BLOOD-MOTION MAN:
WILLIAM HARVEY

Going with the flow In 1628, English doctor William Harvey discovered that the blood system is a single, "closed-loop" system—kind of like an electrical circuit. The blood travels in one direction only, and is pumped around by the heart. Today, this idea seems beyond common sense, but it was totally radical for its time.

HE'S A LIFESAVER:
KARL LANDSTEINER

Blood types In 1901, Landsteiner found that blood comes in different types, and that even people have blood types that are not the same. Many blood types won't mix—instead, they clump and block blood vessels. This science shocker explained why transferring blood from one person to another usually didn't work. It also enabled people to donate their blood for lifesaving operations.

KEY DISCOVERIES

* **Blood circulates (goes around) the whole body as one complete system.**
* **The heart pumps the blood around the body, in one direction only.**
* **The brain and nervous system transmit messages as electrical signals through nerve fibers.**
* **There are different blood types, and many of them won't mix.**
* **Cells from adult organisms can be "encouraged" to transform themselves into stem cells.**

BODY IMAGING

Advances made in the 20th century have changed the way we study the body. Invisible rays, such as X-rays (see page 43), and other medical scanning technologies—known as PET, CAT, and MRI—allow us to look inside the body without the need to cut it open.

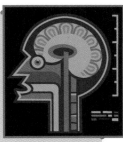

MRI scan of the brain

TWO GREAT MINDS:
GURDON AND YAMANAKA

Reprogramming Stem cells are "magic" cells that can mature into any other type of body cell. Scientists can use them to regrow damaged body parts. They used to be collected from unborn embryos, but Gurdon and Yamanaka proved that adult cells can be "reprogrammed" to go back to being stem cells. To make this breakthrough, Gurdon injected frog eggs with adult frog cell nuclei in 1962. Yamanaka's much later work of 2006 involved tinkering with the genes of skin cells. They were both rewarded with a Nobel Prize in 2012.

THE DIGESTIVE MACHINE

What happens to food between mouth and rear end? Apart from the odd gurgle, the body's internal workings are a mystery. Here is the "inside story" of the fearless food finders who traced the dark ways of the digestive system.

In 1752, René Réaumur tasted his pet buzzard's stomach juices and found them to be very tart (acidic)! Inspired by this, Lazzaro Spallanzani swallowed holey tubes containing food, so that he could pluck them out of his belly and see what had happened to the food. These self-experimenting dudes decided that digestion is a chemical process.

William Beaumont (1785–1853)

Erasistratus (ca. 304–250BCE)

Lazzaro Spallanzani (1729–99)

MECHANICAL MOUTH
The first stage of digesting food is mashing it up with the teeth. Scientists call this "mastication." As well as grinding, softening, and shredding it, the mouth mixes the food with drool. Your spit, or "saliva," contains digestive chemicals called enzymes, which start to break down the food immediately.

FOOD IS CHURNED UP IN THE TUMMY, NOT COOKED.

On average, food stays in the stomach for about 3–3.5 hours.

Swallowed food takes about ten seconds to reach the stomach.

Liver

Stomach

Panc

René Réaumur (1683–1757)

Theodor Schwann (1810–82)

Esophagus (food pipe)

DIGESTIVE STUDIES

Theodor Schwann discovered protein-digesting enzymes. But things really changed when an army doctor, called William Beaumont, found a fur trapper who had been shot in the stomach. Bill was able to dangle food—on a thread—into the trapper's tank, and observe the course of digestion as it happened inside the stomach.

I WAS THE FIRST TO EXTRACT PANCREATIC JUICES, CHEERS!

Regnier de Graaf
(1641–73)

THE SMALL INTESTINE

By now, food is mulched down enough that nutrients and sugars can be taken into the blood. This happens in a tube inside the body's mid-section, which is 16ft (5m) long and lined with millions of tiny fingers called villi. Blood vessels running through the villi absorb goodies into the bloodstream. A forest of strange, digestive bacteria lives in here as well.

The liver and pancreas pump in juices to help break down fat.

BUT IT WAS I WHO FIGURED OUT WHAT THE LIVER AND PANCREAS DO!

Small intestine

Villi
(above)

Large intestine

Claude Bernard
(1813–78)

WEIGHING WASTE

For 30 years, an Italian professor called Santorio Santorio (is there an echo in here ...?) carefully weighed everything that went in and came out of his body. He took all his meals seated on a "balance chair," a contraption that measured the weight of all that he ate and drank. Then he had his assistants weigh his pee and poo. Talk about a rotten job! The Italian found that for every eight pounds (3.6kg) of food he ate, he excreted (pooped) only about three pounds (1.4kg) of waste.

Santorio Santorio
(1561–1636)

PRIVATE

THE LARGE INTESTINE

Anything that the body cannot digest travels down to the large intestine. The big job of the large intestine is to remove water from the solid waste and make, ahem, "big jobs." Poop. This takes about 12 hours, and you'll know when it's done because you'll need a trip to the bathroom!

THE STORY OF MICROBES

NEWS FLASH! We are the aliens on this planet! Earth belongs to tiny life forms we need a microscope to see. We could not live without them—they remove our waste, recycle chemicals, provide us with oxygen, and help plants to grow.

ROBERT HOOKE

World of the tiny Gather 'round boys and girls, moms and dads ... If you lived in the mid-1600s, you couldn't miss Hooke's book. It was called *Micrographia*, and it was the "big thing" of its time, crammed full of marvels such as drawings of fleas, snowflakes, flies' eyes, and plant cells—all seen through a compound microscope. This was most people's first view of the world of very tiny things.

THE FIRST "MICRONAUT":

ANTONIE VAN LEEUWENHOEK

Life through a lens In the 1670s, a curious cloth merchant from the Netherlands stumbled upon a wriggly world that no one had ever seen before. Leeuwenhoek made his own magnifying glasses for checking defects in cloth. When using them to look at some pond water, he spied what he called "cavorting wee beasties"—thousands of times smaller than can be seen with the unaided eye. He had discovered bacteria.

Want to know what a cell is? Learn how life is made of cells on page 31 of the Story of Life Itself.

EARLY MICROLIFE

Since the beginning of life on Earth, this planet has belonged to microlife. The first living things were tiny bacteria that lived in the oceans about 3.8 billion years ago. Made up of just a single cell, these beasties began to make their own food, using energy captured from sunlight. They released oxygen in the process, making the air breathable for larger organisms—and, once we had evolved, for us, too. There are billions upon billions of these single-celled creatures on the planet, living in every nook and cranny—and we don't know half of them or what they really do!

ELECTRON TUNNELERS:

ROHRER AND BINNIG

A new microscope As with light, matter can have wave-like properties (see pages 38–39). Armed with this fact, Swiss spark Heinrich Rohrer and German genius Gerd Binnig used "wavy" electrons to invent a new type of microscope. Their "scanning tunneling" microscope (or STM) can see much smaller things than is possible by using visible light. In 1986, the pair shared a Nobel Prize for their revolutionary work.

Heinrich Rohrer

Gerd Binnig

ROUTE-FINDER

Where did microlife begin? Take a look around on page 35.

Oxygen in the air wasn't discovered until the 1770s. Watch the vicious battle over its discovery on pages 46–47.

There are more microbes in the body than there are cells in the body. See how they aid the process of digesting food on pages 54–55.

Introducing: PASTEUR'S GERM LAB

Here at the world-famous Pasteur Institute in Paris, France, we are on the trail of a gang of nasty offenders responsible for a global "grime wave." With the aid of Louis Pasteur's germ forensics, we'll soon bring an end to their dirty business!

THE WORST OFFENDERS
Here are the Pasteur Institute's most-wanted criminals:

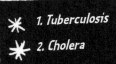

* 1. Tuberculosis
* 2. Cholera
* 3. Anthrax
* 4. Smallpox

Now that we have indentified the rogues, we can hunt those microbes down!

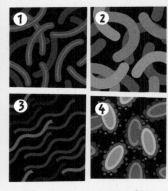

MOST WANTED

Louis Pasteur
(1822–95)

SWAN-NECKED FLASKS
According to Pasteur, it's living things that spoil food and cause disease. His meat-soup experiment proved this! He heated some broth to kill anything in there, then poured it into special flasks. Both jars were open to the air—but the curved "swan neck" trapped anything entering. Louis allowed broth into the bend of the second jar. This one was soon swimming with micro-beasts and went bad, while the first one stayed clean and healthy to eat. *Voila!*

Microbes are trapped in the neck of the first flask.

The microbes can reach the broth in the second flask.

THIS PROVES THAT GERMS DON'T JUST SPRING OUT OF NOWHERE!

SPOILED DRINKS
French sailors of the 19th century were getting upset because their wine was spoiling on sea voyages. Their boss, Napoleon III, asked Pasteur for help. So, Louis invented a method to heat wine—just enough to kill the microbes that were spoiling it, but not enough to ruin the taste. *Salut, mes amis!* ("Cheers!")

MILK
THE FASTEST DRINK ON THE PLANET... IT'S
PAST-YOUR-EYES-ED BEFORE YOU SEE IT!

PASTEURIZED PRODUCTS
Pasteurization is a really important process for lots of products that we enjoy every day. Milk, yogurt, cheese, and beer are normally all pasteurized before they end up in your shopping basket. This makes them stay fresh for longer, which also means less waste—there's no need to throw so many foods and drinks away!

SAVING LIVES
In 1885, Pasteur tracked down a germ in the brain of a dog suffering from a nasty disease called rabies. He then created a "vaccine." This works by exposing a person to a weakened form of the bug, so that he or she can build up a resistance to it without getting the full-blown disease. Pasteur injected the vaccine into a boy who had been bitten by a dog with rabies—and saved his life.

RABIES
LAB

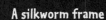
A silkworm frame

SAVING THE SILK TRADE
When silkworms started dying in the south of France, the trade of products made from their fine silk threads was under threat. In 1865, Detective Pasteur triumphed again! Using his trusty microscopes, he discovered the microbes that were attacking the silkworm eggs. Louis also invented a test that helped to detect the disease-causing microbes.

Robert Koch (see page 61) came up with some golden rules for singling out disease-causing germs.

RULE 1: The bugs are where the disease is, so look for your germ in a sick living thing. RULE 2: Isolate the microbe and "culture" (grow) it in a lab. RULE 3: Inject it into a healthy organism—if it's the right germ, it will cause the disease. RULE 4: Make doubly sure by identifying and isolating the nasty germ once again, this time from the newly infected living thing.

EXIT HERE

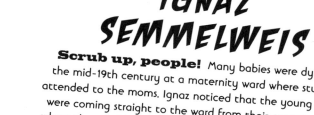

Micro-bugs have got a terrible reputation. It's a little unfair, since a lot of bacteria do good things. However, pathogens—the truly "bad" microbes—make food and water unhealthy, rot our teeth, and make us ill. When the germs attacked, here are the rebels who fought back!

DEAD END

THE "MIASMA THEORY" HAD BEEN AROUND SINCE AROUND THE 1ST CENTURY CE. BECAUSE PEOPLE GOT SICK AROUND FOUL-SMELLING SWAMPS, CESSPITS, AND PILES OF MANURE, THEY THOUGHT DISEASES MUST BE SPREAD BY "BAD AIR" OR POISONOUS GASES KNOWN AS "MIASMAS." WE NOW KNOW THAT THEY'RE SPREAD BY GERMS LIVING IN THE GRIME AND WATER.

DAZZLING DOCTOR:
EDWARD JENNER

Jab, jab! In the 18th century, milkmaids were catching cowpox (a mild disease) from the cows they milked. This seemed to make them immune to a much worse, disfiguring disease called smallpox. In 1796, Jenner put this to the test by deliberately infecting a boy with a jab of cowpox. The following week, Doctor Danger infected the lad with smallpox. Little James didn't get sick. The world's first "vaccination" had protected him against the more dangerous virus.

CLEAN CUSTOMER:
IGNAZ SEMMELWEIS

Scrub up, people! Many babies were dying in the mid-19th century at a maternity ward where students attended to the moms. Ignaz noticed that the young doctors were coming straight to the ward from their anatomy class, where they had been fiddling around inside dead and rotting bodies. He organized a strict hand-cleaning regime at the hospital, and the deaths stopped almost entirely.

GERM TERMINATOR:
ROBERT KOCH

The germ police Once ace German scientist Robert Koch had ridden onto the scene, in the 1870s and '80s, there was no more peace for pathogens. Building on Louis Pasteur's work (see pages 58–59), Koch set the gold standard for research into bugs. He successfully cornered the despicable germs that caused tuberculosis and cholera in humans—two of the most deadly diseases of the day.

KEY DISCOVERIES

* There is a whole world of tiny things, smaller than the human eye can see.

* The bodies of all living things are made out of tiny cells.

* Most of the living things on the planet are tiny bacteria and other microbes.

* Germs (living things) spread disease. Washing and keeping clean can help defeat disease.

* Microbes do helpful things, too.

* Vaccines work by exposing the body to a weaker form of a virus, allowing it to build up an immunity to it.

You look nice today!

FRIENDLY BACTERIA

"Good" bacteria in our guts help us to digest food (see pages 54–55). Their teeny-tiny, bacterial "micro-farts" add together to make your supersonic pants blasts. Bacteria are really important for animals such as cows and sheep, who have an extra stomach for breaking down tough grasses. They produce lots of methane gas. Other bacteria help to ferment milk for making yogurt.

MOLD MAN:
ALEXANDER FLEMING

Dirty dishes Coming back from his vacation, in 1928, Alexander Fleming was amazed to discover a bacteria-killing mold growing in a lab dish that he'd forgotten to clean up. Later, in 1941, Australian Howard Florey and German refugee Ernst Boris Chain developed a drug based on this wonderful green stuff. It was penicillin, the first microbe-killing antibiotic.

THE STORY OF GENETICS

This bunch of gene geniuses went crazy figuring out why living things look like their parents. Together they built an entirely new branch of knowledge about how traits (characteristics) are passed on and shared in families.

DNA PIONEER: FRIEDRICH MIESCHER

Going nuclear Running the extra mile for science, in 1871, Miescher collected pus-filled bandages from a local hospital. Ew! At the heart of each pus cell he found a substance, which he named "nuclein." There was about 6ft (2m) of it in each cell's nucleus. He guessed it had something to do with what gets passed on. We now call this stuff DNA.

GREEN THINKING: GREGOR MENDEL

Yes, peas! In the 1850s and '60s, this Augustinian monk spent a lot of time in the vegetable patch. He was on the trail of what makes parents and offspring so similar. After breeding more than 30,000 pea plants, Mendel figured out that traits get passed on in whole "chunks." But no one was interested.

LIKE PEAS IN A POD

Mendel followed seven traits in his pea plants and traced how they were passed on. He noticed that some traits, such as yellow or green pods, were either "ON" or "OFF"—there was no sharing or mixing.

MENDEL BACK IN VOGUE

In 1900, Hugo de Vries, Carl Correns, and Erich von Tschermak-Seysenegg dusted off Gregor Mendel's "laws of inheritance." Their experiments showed that he was right on the ball!

MY WORD! In a letter in 1905, British scientist William Bateson (1861–1926) came up with the word "genetics."

CODE-BREAKER:
FREDERICK GRIFFITH

Bacterial borrowers In 1928, Fred Griffith discovered that harmless bacteria could "borrow" nasty parts from dead bacteria. They could even pass the same stuff on to their offspring! This was deeply weird. Griffith figured the information the bacteria were getting hold of was somehow "coded" on the DNA of the chromosomes!

BLITZED RESEARCH!
Griffith's investigations were tragically cut short on the night of April 17, 1941, when he and research colleague William M. Scott were killed in a bombing raid on London, UK.

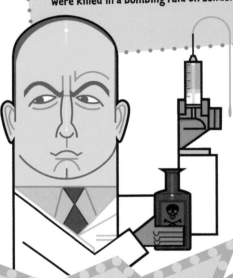

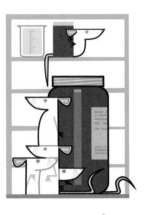

SUPER-FLY GUY:
THOMAS HUNT MORGAN

The eyes have it This guy closed in on genes in 1910. His experiments on fruit flies proved that the stuff that gets passed from parents to offspring is on the "chromosomes," strands of nuclein that are copied when a cell divides. Morgan linked the flies with white eyes to the "X" chromosome.

A BIG LEAP!

In 1944, Canadian-born scientist Oswald Avery repeated Griffith's experiments and proved that it's DNA—and not the cell proteins—that gets passed from generation to generation. But HOW does this happen?

FACE-OFF: CRICK, WATSON, AND WILKINS VS. ROSALIND FRANKLIN

DNA DISPUTE

The time: 1952–53. The battleground: England, UK. Two teams are chasing the BIG QUESTION in science: what's the shape of the DNA molecule? At stake is global fame and science superstardom. In the King's College London corner are Rosalind Franklin and Maurice Wilkins; in the Cambridge University corner, Francis Crick and James Watson. It's a science scrap, a DNA dustup—FIGHT!!

THE TWEED AVENGER:
FRANCIS CRICK

"**Greetings.** Young Watson and I are math and physics whizzes by training, but why not tackle the BIG Questions wherever they may be found? They warned us about DNA——but when the prize is the secret of life itself, you've got to be in it to win it. We are winners, not quitters, and *no one* makes molecular models like we do!"

THE MATH MAVERICK:
JAMES D. WATSON

"**Hey, y'all!** I went to college at 16 and got my PhD aged 22! Then I left the USA and came to England to make some waves. The sky's the limit, and I'm not above a little petty theft when it's in the name of science. We just need that lil' something from Rosie. Without our 'help' she'll never spot DNA's secret spiral structure!"

PHOTO 51

"X-ray crystallography" is a way of revealing the structure of a crystal by shining a beam of X-rays through it. Taken in 1952 by Rosalind Franklin's lab team, Photo 51 was the KEY piece of X-ray evidence for the structure of DNA. The Cambridge duo were desperate to see it, so Franklin kept it locked away. But the wily Wilkins got hold of it and showed it to Watson.

DARK DNA LADY:
ROSALIND FRANKLIN

*"**Bah!!** I'm sick of this bullying boy's club. You won't let me use the lunchroom? Fine, prepare to see how powerful a female academic can be. I have the best DNA samples available—I just need peace and time to do real science. I've got no time for fame-hungry wannabes! You see, no one else has my world-class X-ray imaging skills. POW!"*

MISTER X-RAY:
MAURICE WILKINS

*"**Oh, dear.** It's all a terrible misunderstanding. I'm in a frightful state. I thought the old gal Rosie was working for me, but she has her own ideas, and by golly, she doesn't hesitate to let me know! Those decent fellows at Cambridge are much more my type. I say, chaps, have you seen this lovely little photograph?"*

THE WINNERS

In April 1953, Crick and Watson revealed that DNA is a "double helix"—a twirling double strand that looks like a twisted rope ladder. Untangling its structure shows how life stores its secrets in a nonliving molecule. DNA is a complete set of blueprints for any living thing and sits inside the heart of each cell. Crick, Watson, and Wilkins won a Nobel Prize in 1962. Poor Rosalind Franklin missed out because she died in 1958.

LIFE'S RECIPE BOOK

DNA is a complete instruction manual (or blueprint) for a living organism. The instructions for a human are about 800 times the length of the Bible.

DNA DETECTIVE:
ALEC JEFFREYS

Genetic fingerprints Alec Jeffreys' *Eureka!* moment came along in 1984, when he saw that everybody's "junk DNA" (the parts of a genome that aren't genes) is unique. Criminals always leave something behind at a crime scene—a strand of hair, an eyelash, or even blood—and, just like a fingerprint, the DNA it contains is enough to identify them.

TOP IN HER FIELD:
BARBARA McCLINTOCK

Jumping genes This scientist spent her life studying corn-on-the-cob. No one believed McClintock when she spotted genes that moved places on a chromosome and caused unusual color patterns. But Barbara was a born rebel and she stuck to her claims. Eventually, in 1983, she was awarded a Nobel Prize for her discovery. Now "jumping genes" are used to study genetic diseases. Nothing "corny" about that, eh?!

SERVICE STATION

The discovery of the structure of DNA was just the start of the story. Once scientists understood the secret of the molecule's double spiral, they could not only read its code, but also start to find out what genes do and how they work.

IN 1975, A BIG BRAINIAC CALLED FREDERICK SANGER (1918–2013) INVENTED A QUICK METHOD FOR "READING" DNA CODE, KNOWN AS SEQUENCING. SANGER IS THE ONLY PERSON TO HAVE WON *TWO* NOBEL PRIZES IN CHEMISTRY.

DNA IS READ IN THREES

In 1961, Francis Crick and Sydney Brenner figured out that the "words" in DNA codes are read in triplets (groups of three "base pairs"). Genes are like "sentences" of DNA code. Like telegrams, they have a sequence that reads "STOP" at the end.

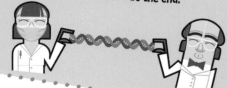

THE HUMAN GENOME PROJECT

An international project to make a map of every human gene turned into a bad-tempered race, when Craig Venter's private research company went head-to-head with the National Center for Human Genome Research. What was supposed to be a 15-year amble was finished in a 2-year sprint. The result was a grumpy "tie" in 2000.

KEY DISCOVERIES

* Traits are inherited in whole chunks called genes, and are not mixed together.

* DNA is in a cell's nucleus.

* DNA has a "double helix" spiral structure.

* Genes are on the DNA chromosomes.

* Humans have about 20,000 genes.

* Our non-coding "junk" DNA can identify us.

MAVERICK MAP-MAKER:
FRANCIS COLLINS

Rising star The Human Genome Project's (HGP) head honcho completed the genome of yeast in 1996—the first genome of a living thing with a cell nucleus. HGP and Venter's company, Celera, jointly released the human genome in 2003, on the 50th anniversary of the discovery of the structure of DNA.

GENE DESIGNER:
CRAIG VENTER

Shotgun science Using a piledriver technique called "shotgun sequencing," dirtbike devil Craig Venter was able to decipher DNA codes much faster than any of his rivals—and at bargain prices. In 1995, his Celera Genomics company released the first complete genome map of a free-living organism.

DNA DROPOUT:
KARY MULLIS

Quick copies Maverick Mullis invented a chemical reaction that acts like a photocopier for genes. Using Mullis's "polymerase chain reaction" (PCR), "thermocyclers" allow scientists to run off as much DNA as they want in just a few hours. Thermocyclers are now standard equipment for every genetics and forensics lab.

Introducing: A BRAVE NEW WORLD

Spinning his science records tonight: it's rogue remixer and gene reshuffler extraordinaire, Craig Venter! When this kingpin, this giant of genomics, ain't racin' his dirtbike or riding his speedboat, he's makin' waves in the wild world of synthetic biology. Whaddaguy!

GENETIC REMIXING

Using special proteins called restriction enzymes, genetic remixers can isolate a gene and snip out its strip of DNA. They then knit this strand into the DNA fabric of another living thing to give it desirable traits. The genetic message is loaded into a "vector"—a bacterium or virus—which invades cells and smuggles in the foreign DNA.

YO! I'M THE NUMBER-ONE CUT-AND-PASTE MIX-MASTER!

GENETICALLY MODIFIED ORGANISMS (GMOs)

GMOs are living things that have never existed before on Earth. They are made by carefully remixing an organism's genes while it is still a microscopic egg cell. By splicing in genes from other living things, the new organism "borrows" traits (unique characteristics) that give it superpowers.

CRAIG'S GMO PLAYLIST (KEY)

1. Cold-weather-resistant crops
2. Pest-proof plants
3. "Pharming": animals that produce drugs
4. Animals bred for research
5. Bumper-crop plants

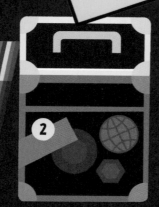

FLUORESCENT DAZZLERS

The green fluorescent protein (GFP) gene produces a chemical that glows in bright, fluorescent colors under an ultraviolet light. Originally taken from a jellyfish, it's used as a "reporter gene" in tests to see if the newly spliced "rDNA" is working. If all is functioning properly, the GFP pumps out its crazy shades of color.

IT'S A FLUORESCENT DNA DISCO! TOTALLY PSYCHEDELIC!

SYNTHETIC ORGANISMS

The boy Venter's special hobby is building life from the ground up. If you can find the minimum number of genes necessary for life, you can then design and build—using a computer—genomes never before seen in nature! Venter calls this "Life 2.0."

"Synthia": the world's first synthetic organism

CREATING A CLONE

Clones are living things that have *exactly* the same genetic makeup as their parents. This is not always an artificial process. Growing a houseplant from a leaf cutting is a *natural* form of cloning. Cloning large animals in the lab has not been very successful—but this is how it's done.

THE CELL NUCLEUS IS EXTRACTED

1. Take an egg cell. Suck out its nucleus and swap it for one from the cell of the animal you want to clone.

THE CELL DIVIDES

2. With special care, you can coax this modified cell into dividing and growing just like a normal, fertilized egg cell.

DEVELOPED EMBRYO IS IMPLANTED

MOTHER GIVES BI[RTH] TO IDENTICAL CL[ONE]

3. Implant the devel[oped] embryo into a moth[er] and wait until the c[lone is] born in the usual wa[y.]

THE STORY OF THE QUANTUM WORLD

These rebels ripped up the old rule books of physics. They delved deep into the world inside the atom—farther than anyone had gone before—and found a new reality that had confusing and sometimes crazy rules. Prepare yourself for quantum weirdness.

INVISIBLE HEAT

All hot things give off electromagnetic energy. The hotter they get, the greater the energy of the radiation. People and objects at room temperature give off invisible, infrared rays (see page 42). Thermal imaging cameras can sense this kind of "body heat" radiation to spot people: for example, if they've been trapped under snow or rubble.

RELUCTANT REVOLUTIONARY:
MAX PLANCK

Hot bodies Max Planck never wanted to rock the boat, but old-school physics just couldn't explain thermal radiation—how we feel heat from a fire even when the air (in between the fire and us) is cold. Max tore up the old ideas in 1900, saying that the radiation comes in fixed packets of energy. He also invented the term "quantum" to refer to each energy packet. This was the start of a major revolution in physics.

Go to page 72 to see how Einstein used Planck's "quantum" brainwave to say that light comes in energy "packets."

THE BIG BOOK OF **CLASSICAL PHYSICS**

THE GREAT DANE:
NIELS BOHR

The quantum atom By 1913, Niels Bohr (see page 23) had realized that even the energies of electrons in atoms are set into "fixed" levels. In other words, they are "quantized." Electrons can absorb energy to make a "quantum leap" to a higher energy level, and they emit a photon of light when they drop back down. This keeps atoms so steady and stable that they last forever and ever.

THE NOBLE PHYSICIST:
LOUIS DE BROGLIE

Waves of matter After Albert Einstein had shown that photons of light come as both waves and particles (see page 39), a French nobleman called Louis de Broglie went one step further. If matter and light are both quantum in nature, then they can both be described as waves. Like the vibrations on a violin string, electrons have wave-like properties, too. The higher energies vibrate more quickly, just like high-pitched musical notes.

ROUTE-FINDER

Watch Niels Bohr "cook up" his quantum atom on page 23.

Take a look through the incredible "scanning tunneling" microscope on page 57.

Turn the page to see Einstein's awesome discoveries on pages 72–73.

SUPERCONDUCTIVITY

When certain materials get very chilly, their electrical resistance disappears. With zero resistance to electrical currents, these "superconductors" can create powerful magnetic fields. The effect is sometimes strong enough to cause an object to rise and hover, as if by magic, above the superconductive material. Discovered in 1911, this "quantum mechanical effect" can't be explained by traditional laws of physics.

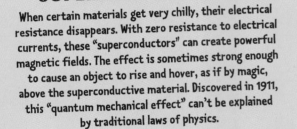

Introducing:
A RELATIVE GENIUS

If you're a fan of quantum insanity, today is your lucky day! Albert Einstein, the most famous scientist of all time, turned everything upside down and helped to rewrite the books of physics. And he has agreed to take you on a tour of his best moments.

SPECIAL RELATIVITY

Einstein felt that the laws of physics shouldn't change, no matter what. He said that light always travels at the same speed for every observer, no matter how fast each observer is moving. Even if you were traveling near to light speed, you'd still see your reflection in a mirror. That means that time must run at different rates for people traveling at different speeds.

> MY EXPERIMENTS WERE "THOUGHT EXPERIMENTS" THAT I DID IN MY HEAD.

The photoelectric effect is used in night-vision goggles.

Incoming beam of light.

The electrons are knocked off of a metal surface.

THE PHOTOELECTRIC EFFECT

This is a strange effect where light knocks electrons off the surface of materials. The effect suggested to Einstein that light is made of individual "packets" of energy. He called these chunks—or "quanta"—photons. The energy of each photon is related to its frequency (the number of waves per second).

> MAKE EVERYTHING AS SIMPLE AS POSSIBLE, BUT NOT SIMPLER.

Relativity says that time is relative. We all have our personal time. So, as this spacecraft approaches the speed of light (186,282 miles/ 299,292,458m per second), time runs more slowly for its occupants.

MONSTER BRAIN

German über-genius Albert Einstein (1879–1955) was a fabulously rebellious scientist. In science, there are often things that can't be easily explained. Rather than dismissing the effects of experiments that didn't fit neatly with what was thought to be true, Einstein believed that the *results* were good and the *theories* were probably wrong.

Zany revolutionary Einstein was the model of a mad scientist. His ideas are famously hard to understand, but he always encouraged people to reach out further. He said, "Anyone who has never made a mistake has never tried anything new."

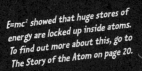

$E=mc^2$ showed that huge stores of energy are locked up inside atoms. To find out more about this, go to The Story of the Atom on page 20.

RELATIVE WEIRDNESS
Relativity creates some odd effects, such as time *slowing down* for anyone traveling close to the speed of light. In Einstein's "twin paradox," one twin travels close to the speed of light, and then returns to find that he has aged less than his brother. Time went by more slowly for the moving twin.

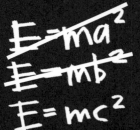

$$E=ma^2$$
$$E=mb^2$$
$$E=mc^2$$

MATTER-ENERGY EQUIVALENCE
Albert's famous equation $E=mc^2$ shows that matter and energy are different sides of the same coin. Each one can be converted into the other.

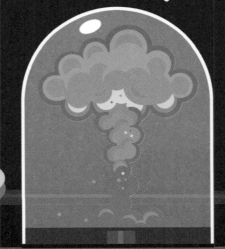

EXIT HERE

WAVE MECHANIC:
ERWIN SCHRÖDINGER

Cats and waves ... Erwin's big ambition was to build a solid framework for this new kind of physics. In 1926, using old elements of math, he made up an amazing equation for describing matter as a wave. But this "quantum mechanic" was very unhappy with his creation because it gave outrageous, weird results—such as saying things could be in two places at once!

QUANTUM TOOLBOX

CASINO

The deeper inside matter the quantum explorers went, the weirder the situation got. Down in the land of the subatomic particles, things just don't appear to work the same way as they do in the everyday world. Our best scientists are still trying to figure out why.

AN UNCERTAIN MAN:
WERNER HEISENBERG

The uncertainty principle In 1927, Heisenberg realized that it's pointless trying to predict the position of an electron—and other particles—because there will always be an uncertainty attached to its position or velocity (speed). He thought Schrödinger was OCD—rather than sweat over which outcome was the correct one, why not accept all possibilities? However unlikely, maybe it's better to assume that *anything* can happen!

QUANTUM WEIRDNESS

Many strange things are allowed in the quantum world—things that make no sense. Particles can be in two places at the same time and can appear on the other side of unscalable walls, seeming to tunnel magically through them. These insane events are crucial to the way transistors and "semiconductor" computer chips work.

THE TROUBLESHOOTER:
H. DIETER ZEH

A quantum leap Zeh came up with a theory that got quantum scientists out of a fairly sticky spot in 1970. Their equations say bizarre things that happen that no one can actually see. For example, quantum theory says that the toss of a coin can come up as both heads and tails, but we only ever *see* one or the other outcome. Zeh's "decoherence" explains how our non-crazy, ordinary world arises from the totally weird, quantum world.

Laser light was an idea of Einstein's (see pages 72–73). It depends on the "quantization" of energy levels in the atom (see page 71) and was invented by Charles H. Townes (see page 39).

KEY DISCOVERIES

* **Energy comes in chunks or "packets" of energy called quanta. A quantum of light is called a photon.**

* **The energy in an atom is also "quantized." Particles of matter act like waves.**

* **All quantum interactions can be thought of as waves.**

* **There is no way of knowing the outcome of a quantum interaction before it happens.**

* **Quantum physics has taught us that there is a huge amount still to be discovered about the true nature of our reality.**

GLOSSARY

ALPHA PARTICLE A heavy particle made of two protons and two neutrons, sent flying out of an unstable (radioactive) atomic nucleus when it decays.

ANTIBIOTIC A bacteria-killing substance. Antibiotic drugs help your body to fight infections.

ATOM The smallest part of matter. Atoms make up all the things you can see around you. Atoms are made of protons, neutrons, and electrons. Different types of atoms are called elements.

ATOMIC NUMBER The number of protons in an atom. Heavier atoms have more protons.

BACTERIUM (PLURAL: BACTERIA) Smaller than the eye can see, these tiny living things have only one cell. They were some of the first things to live on Earth.

BLACK SMOKER A deep-sea "chimney" on the ocean floor. The "smoke" is actually superheated water coming up from below Earth's crust—and it is crammed full of minerals. Also known as a hydrothermal vent.

CARBON DIOXIDE A gas that is breathed out by humans, as a waste product. Plants use the gas when they convert energy from the Sun to make food.

CELL A tiny bag of chemicals surrounded by a protective wall. Cells are known as "the building blocks of life" because all living things are made out of them. They contain DNA and can make copies of themselves. The human body has about 100 trillion cells.

CHAIN REACTION A nuclear chain reaction powers atomic bombs and nuclear reactors. Each time an atomic nucleus splits, it releases more neutrons that can go on to split other nuclei, creating a "domino effect."

CHROMOSOME Strands of coiled DNA that carry genes. They are bunched up tightly in a cell's nucleus.

COMPOUND A substance created when two or more elements combine chemically.

CRUST The solid, rocky outer layer of the Earth. The crust is broken up into tectonic plates.

DECAY When the nucleus of an unstable atom breaks down, it releases energy as nuclear radiation—alpha and beta particles, and gamma rays. Nuclear decay makes atoms change from one element into another.

DENSITY A measure of how compressed or squashed a material is. Density is the mass of matter found in a certain volume (three-dimensional area) of space.

DNA A twisted, double-strand molecule that holds the coded instructions for building and running a living thing. DNA is stored in the nucleus of a cell.

ELECTROMAGNETIC RADIATION A form of energy that travels through space as waves and particles called photons. EM radiation travels at the speed of light and includes radio, infrared, visible light, ultraviolet, X-rays, and gamma rays.

ELECTROMAGNETISM (EM) The forces of attraction and repulsion that occur between electrical charges, due to electric and magnetic fields.

ELECTRON A very tiny, light, negatively charged subatomic particle that zips around the outer regions of an atom, orbiting the positively charged atomic nucleus.

ELEMENT A chemically pure substance made of just one type of atom. There are 118 known elements.

EMBRYO The earliest stage of development after a fertilized egg cell first divides into two and begins to grow. This stage in humans lasts about eight weeks.

ENZYME A non-living chemical that helps to control the rate, or speed, of life processes in the body.

FREQUENCY A count of the number of complete up-and-down wobbles a wave makes in the space of a certain time period, measured in cycles per second.

GENE A set of chemical instructions for how to build and run a human body, coded in DNA and stored on chromosomes in the cell nucleus. Everyone has two sets of genes: one from a mother and one from a father.

GENOME The complete set of DNA in the body. Genomes are made up of coded genetic instructions (genes) and the non-coding parts of DNA.

GERM A disease-carrying microbe.

GLOBAL WARMING The rise in the average temperature of the planet. The largest push toward higher temperatures comes from the greenhouse gas carbon dioxide—released into the atmosphere by burning fossil fuels (naturally occurring materials).

GRAVITY The invisible force of attraction between all objects that have mass.

HOMINID The family of great apes that includes humans, chimpanzees, gorillas, orangutans, and their ancestors (related species from the past).

IMMUNITY A resistance to infection or disease.

INHERITANCE The traits that are passed from a parent to a child. Your genes are a "new combination" taken from the genes of both of your parents.

JUNK DNA The parts of the genome that are not genes. These DNA sequences are more properly called "non-coding" DNA. They look like useless nonsense, but they may play a role we do not yet fully understand.

MAGNETIC FIELD An invisible force field of magnetic attraction (and repulsion) surrounding a magnet or electrical current moving in a conductor.

MANTLE The gloopy layer of hot, liquid rocks that lies underneath Earth's crust. The tectonic plates "float" on this as they move across the planet's surface.

MASS A measure of the amount of matter, or stuff, that makes up an object or substance.

MATTER Matter is made of atoms. It has mass, and it is visible. Because it has mass, matter feels the force of gravity. It exists as a solid, liquid, gas, or plasma.

MICROBE A microscopic living thing, such as a bacterium, virus, protist, or fungus. Also called a germ.

MOLECULE A large compound made of more than one atom bonded together. Molecules are the smallest units of any substance, and are the parts that get involved in chemical reactions.

NERVOUS SYSTEM The system of tiny nerve cells and fibers that carry nerve signals (information) around the body as electrical pulses.

NEURON A single nerve cell.

NEUTRON A heavy, subatomic particle—with no electrostatic charge—found in the nucleus of an atom. Neutrons help to bind repelling protons together.

NUCLEUS (PLURAL: NUCLEI) The central part of something. The nucleus of an atom is made of protons and neutrons, and contains nearly all of an atom's mass.

NUTRIENT A substance that provides nourishment for living things and helps them to grow.

ORGANISM All living things are organisms: from single-celled bacteria to multicelled plants and animals.

OVUM An egg cell, made in the body of a female, containing a half-set of chromosomes.

PARTICLE A small part of matter. Protons, neutrons, and electrons are subatomic particles (smaller than atoms) that make up atoms; protons and neutrons are made of even tinier particles known as quarks.

PATHOGEN A disease-causing bacterium, virus, or other microorganism.

PHOTON A small packet of electromagnetic radiation (light energy).

PROTON A heavy, positively charged subatomic particle found in the nucleus of an atom.

QUANTUM (PLURAL: QUANTA) A packet of energy of a fixed and unchanging value.

QUARK One of the basic parts of matter, quarks are the tiny particles that make up protons and neutrons.

RADIATION A "zap" of energy that can travel across the vacuum of space.

RADIOACTIVITY The breakdown of an atom's nucleus, which releases alpha particles, beta particles, or gamma rays. Unstable atoms are "radioactive."

rDNA Stands for "recombinant DNA"—new genetic materials made from strands of DNA spliced together.

REPORTER GENE A gene that is spliced into a newly created strand of rDNA. When the rDNA is working, the reporter gene is "switched on" and signals that it's working by releasing detectable proteins.

REPRODUCTION Sexual reproduction is the process that creates new living things by fusing the sex cells and combining the genes from a male and a female of the same species (type) of organism.

SPERM A sex cell, produced in the body of a male, containing a half-set of chromosomes.

TRAIT Genetic characteristics that are passed down from generation to generation. Traits that are matched to certain genes are inherited from one or both parents.

VACCINE A substance, usually a weakened form of a pathogen, that encourages the body's immune (defense) system to build up a resistance to a disease. Vaccines are usually given as an injection, or "shot."

VACUUM A space that is empty of all matter.

VECTOR A bacterium that can invade a cell and transfer its genetic material (DNA) into it. Bacteria or viruses are used as vectors to make rDNA.

VIRUS A nonliving strand of DNA that can invade living cells, hijack their duplication machinery, and force them to pump out multiple copies of the invading virus. People get sick when their bodies are infected by viruses.

WAVE (OF ENERGY) A way in which energy moves from place to place—either by disturbing the particles inside a substance (as with sound and water waves) or by creating an electromagnetic disturbance to travel through a vacuum (as with light and other forms of EM radiation).

WEIGHT The measure of gravity's effect on an object's mass. Objects with more mass have a greater gravitational attraction to the planet, and so they feel heavier and weigh more.

INDEX